" *A fresh new take on the subtleties of writing great fiction. Mike Klaassen's guide should be on every fiction writer's shelf.*

— EVAN MARSHALL, AUTHOR OF *THE MARSHALL PLAN®*
FOR NOVEL WRITING

" *I like Mike Klaassen's Fiction Writing Modes a lot. It's a damn good book.*

— JAMES N. FREY, AUTHOR OF *HOW TO WRITE A DAMN GOOD NOVEL*

" *One of the most definitive, well-researched approaches to writing fiction that I've ever read. Mike Klaassen has the essential desk reference for fiction writers. Stop what you're writing; read this book, and get ready to apply his eleven modes before you get back to your manuscript. This book will reinvent your writing.*

— JAMES V. SMITH, JR., AUTHOR OF *YOU CAN WRITE A NOVEL*

Mike Klaassen has taken a creative and original approach in his book about using eleven modes to write stories that communicate effectively with readers. I've never seen this approach to storytelling covered anywhere else, and I can see just how practical and helpful it can be to new writers and advanced writers alike.

— GLORIA KEMPTON, AUTHOR OF *DIALOGUE: TECHNIQUES AND EXERCISES FOR CRAFTING EFFECTIVE DIALOGUE (WRITE GREAT FICTION SERIES)*

If you're looking for the tools that will help you create credible, excellent fiction, look no further. Mike's guide to writing fiction is your light at the end of the tunnel. Stop saying 'I wish I could write a book' and just do it! With Mike's help, you are sure to get there.

— MICHAEL LEVIN, *NEW YORK TIMES* BESTSELLING AUTHOR AND CEO OF BUSINESSGHOST

Mike Klaassen has created a valuable addition to the working writer's library with his innovative book, Fiction-Writing Modes. In it, Klaassen goes beyond most craft books in that he's not only identified eleven writing modes —several of which will be new to readers—but also defines them thoroughly and illustrates how writers can use them to create effective fiction. Highly recommended.

— LES EDGERTON, AUTHOR OF *FINDING YOUR VOICE, HOOKED,* AND A NUMBER NOVELS AND NONFICTION WORKS

FICTION-WRITING MODES

ELEVEN ESSENTIAL TOOLS FOR BRINGING YOUR
STORY TO LIFE

MIKE KLAASSEN

TABLE OF CONTENTS

Acknowledgments   7
Preface   9
Note to Readers   15

Part I
INTERIORITY
1. Sensation   23
2. Emotion   37
3. Introspection   55
4. Recollection   71

Part II
ACTIVITY
5. Action   81
6. Summarization   99

Part III
DIALOGUE
7. Conversation   107
8. Advancing Plot Through Action and Dialogue   113
9. Dialogue to Increase Conflict   119
10. Identifying the Speaker   127
11. Verbs and Adverbs of Attribution   133
12. Using Attributions to Control Rhythm and Pace   141
13. Making Dialogue Sound Natural   151
14. Punctuating Dialogue   161

Part IV
EXTERIORITY
15. Narration   175
16. Description   181
17. Exposition   199
18. Transition   207

Part V

OVER THE RAINBOW

19. New Perspectives   225

Explore Other Works By Mike Klaassen   231
About the Author   233
Index   235
Bibliography   241
Endnotes   245

ACKNOWLEDGMENTS

The art and craft of writing fiction has been studied at least since the time of Aristotle. Much has been added to the body of knowledge since the advent of the modern novel just a few hundred years ago. Students of fiction are fortunate to have instructors, agents, authors, and editors who share what they have learned about fiction and the craft of writing it.

In writing this book, I have attempted to present a comprehensive overview of fiction-writing modes. In doing so, I have naturally drawn upon the extensive body of knowledge already in existence. In addition to sources acknowledged in the bibliography, numerous seminars and workshops attended over many years provided a wealth of information.

This book is largely a compilation of the concepts, observations, and recommendations of others. Wherever I have used the exact words of others or paraphrased their words, I have included appropriate attribution. In a body of knowledge as extensive as the craft of writing fiction, much information is repeated and duplicated in many different sources. Identifying the original source of many concepts is challenging, if not impossible. If I have overlooked appropriate attribution, I sincerely apologize.

A natural byproduct of organizing information and writing a manuscript is recognizing new concepts and relationships. Sometimes, that new information contradicts widely accepted conventions. Wherever I felt it appropriate, I included such information and hope it contributes, at least modestly, to the understanding of fiction and the craft of creating it.

I am also grateful to the people at Helium.com, who first published my article "Fiction-writing modes and how to use them" on June 6, 2007.

I have been fortunate over many years to receive guidance from an experienced editor who patiently wades through my work and recommends improvements. This manuscript benefited immensely from the unparalleled guidance of independent editor Laurie Rosin.

I also wish to acknowledge the contribution of my wife of thirty-five years, Carol S. Klaassen (1951-2012), who inspired and encouraged me and was also the first reader of early drafts of the manuscript.

PREFACE

Why, you might ask, would anyone write a book about fiction-writing modes? A *mode* is a particular manner of doing or expressing something. I believe eleven different modes comprise all written fiction. This book describes them and how to use each one effectively. With a deeper understanding of these modes, you can better utilize your creative talents to craft successful fiction.

Fiction writers use these modes to tell stories. No doubt you're already familiar with some of them. *Dialogue* is a mode of fiction writing. So is *narration*. You can probably name a few more, such as *exposition, summarization,* and *description.* The others may be new to you: *recollection, sensation, emotion, introspection, action,* and *transition.*

This book will teach you what you need to know about all eleven and how to use them. You will find that this book is unlike any you have ever read. Other instruction books, however helpful, lack order and a classification system of what comprises written fiction. They do not adequately address all you need to know about fiction-writing modes to become an effective fiction writer. Some articles, books, and seminars identify a few modes, but none of them discuss or even identify all of them.

Were you surprised to learn that there are *eleven* fiction-writing modes? If you don't know the eleven, you may be writing without all the tools available to you. That's the equivalent of a painter trying to create masterpieces with only a few colors.

Learning to write better fiction is an ongoing pursuit. Ernest Hemingway said, "We are all apprentices in a craft where no one ever becomes a master."[1] While that may be true, each of us can *improve* by learning when, where, and how to utilize the basic tools of our craft.

I'm a published author of two young-adult novels, and I publish a fiction-writing newsletter for a growing list of subscribers. I teach writing at seminars and workshops, and I write articles about the craft of writing fiction.

Who should read this book? If you're a beginner, this book will provide an invaluable foundation from which to build your skills. If you're an experienced author, this book may help you reach new levels of success. If you are already a bestselling novelist, you might find interesting the words of Stephen King in the foreword to his book *On Writing: A Memoir of the Craft*: "Fiction writers, present company included, don't understand very much about what they do—not why it works when it's good, not why it doesn't when it's bad."[2] A better understanding of fiction-writing modes can help any writer understand why some writing works and some doesn't.

Writing fiction is not just an *art*. It is also a *craft*. If you want to excel at the craft of writing fiction, you need more than inspiration and intuition. You need skill, and skill comes from know-how. Knowing how to use fiction-writing modes can help you engage a reader, say what you mean, and achieve your intended results. The eleven fiction-writing modes are the tools of an author's trade.

This book will teach you the features, strengths, and weaknesses of each mode. You'll learn the mechanics of writing in each mode. You'll see when to use one mode and not another. You'll master selecting the exact fiction-writing mode for a particular passage to cause the desired effect on the reader.

Let's define the modes first, each of which we'll discuss in depth in the upcoming chapters.

- *Sensation* is the mode for evoking the five senses (sight, hearing, touch, smell, and taste).
- *Emotion* is the mode for relating how a character feels.
- *Introspection* is the mode for sharing a character's thinking.
- *Recollection* is the mode for revealing what a character remembers.
- *Action* is the mode for showing things happening, in detail, as they occur.
- *Summarization* is the mode of restating actions or events.
- *Conversation* is the mode for presenting characters talking.
- *Narration* is the mode by which the narrator communicates directly to the reader.
- *Description* is the mode for portraying people, places, things, or concepts.
- *Exposition* is the mode for conveying information.
- *Transition* is the mode for moving from one place, time, or character to another.

While researching fiction-writing modes and drafting related articles for my monthly online newsletter, *For Fiction Writers*, I formulated ideas to make this book the most comprehensive and concise resource available anywhere regarding fiction-writing modes and the mechanics of presenting them.

This book is about a specific aspect of writing fiction, but having a big-picture understanding is helpful. I believe five fundamental elements comprise all fiction: character, plot, setting, theme, and style. Each has its own specific function within a story:

1. *Plot* is the *what* (or *what happens*).
2. *Character* is the *who.*
3. *Setting* is the *where* and *when.*
4. *Theme* is the *why.*
5. *Style* is the *how.*

All eleven fiction-writing modes apply to the five elements of fiction. Action and summarization are at the core of plot, revealing events in detail or in summary. Sensation, emotion, introspection, and recollection take readers into the mind of our characters, sharing feelings, thoughts, and memories—revealing who each character really is. Description helps us visualize a setting from the tiniest details to the grand vistas of the story's world. Any or all of the eleven modes may contribute to the underlying message of a story's themes.

Fiction-writing modes fit under the element of *style. Style* reflects the myriad of choices fiction writers make in creating fiction. They encompass strategic decisions such as point of view and choosing a narrator, but they also include nitty-gritty, tactical choices of grammar, punctuation, word usage, sentence and paragraph length and structure, tone, imagery, chapter selection, titles, and (drum roll) fiction-writing modes. In the process of creating a story, these choices meld to become the *writer's voice*, his or her unique style. How you use fiction-writing modes and the skill with which you use them becomes a significant aspect of your writing style.

The state of the art of writing fiction is evolving. Your own skill as an author grows as you acquire knowledge. One way to improve your writing capabilities is to learn the components of fiction and how best to use them. This book will help you get closer to writing at your full potential.

Throughout the book's five parts, I include examples to illustrate the issues being addressed. Many examples are drawn from whatever books were within reach as I wrote the manuscript. Some of the examples are from my own young-adult novels, *The Brute* and *Cracks*.

Full disclosure: my preferred writing style is a third-person point of view with a close perspective. I strive for intimate, immediate fiction (terms we will define later). Fiction-writing modes apply to all types of fiction, but my recommendations and examples favor writing in a style favored in thrillers and other popular fiction.

What is the best way to use this book? That depends upon your needs. Reading this book from beginning to end is probably most beneficial, but you may find other ways. If you have a particular interest or writing issue to deal with, look at the table of contents or thumb through the index to locate that specific subject. This book may also be a handy desk reference for answering your questions while you are writing fiction. The various chapters may also serve as inspiration to presentations at writing classes, clubs, and workshops.

Each chapter addresses a fiction-writing mode and how that mode works. This book is intended to be the most comprehensive yet concise discussion about fiction-writing modes anywhere. Some of the information may be familiar to you, but much of it won't.

As far back as I can remember, I've heard the training adage: "See one. Do one. Teach one." I've read fiction, written fiction, and taught fiction. Teaching fiction, including writing this book, helps me become a better writer. I'm pleased to share what I've learned.

NOTE TO READERS

THE EVOLUTION OF FICTION-WRITING MODES

(Adapted from "Fiction-Writing Modes and How to Use Them"
by Mike Klaassen
published by Helium.com on June 6, 2007)

When I first began writing fiction years ago, I was bewildered by the jargon used to describe novels and the process of creating them. Let's face it: There's a lot of information out there, and much of it is conflicting. Year by year, book by book, I've sorted out the terms, structures, and processes needed to turn an idea into a novel.

One day I had a breakthrough in understanding how writing fiction works. I suspect we have all had "aha!" moments when something changes how we look at things. Such a moment for me was many years ago when I was reading *The Marshall Plan for Novel Writing* by Evan Marshall.

One of the keys to successful fiction, according to Marshall, is to know what you're doing and why at all times. He noticed that many beginning novelists don't seem completely conscious of what they're writing. As a result, they misuse what he described as the *fiction-writing modes*—the types of writing of which all fiction is made.[1]

Marshall listed five fiction-writing modes: action, summary, dialogue, feelings/thoughts, and background, each with its own set of conventions regarding how, when, and where it should be used. Over the years I've incorporated them into my writing and my thinking.

Another "aha!" moment occurred when I read Jessica Page Morrell's *Between the Lines: Mastering the Subtle Elements of Fiction Writing*. She listed six *delivery modes*: action, exposition, description, dialogue, summary, and transition.[2]

To their credit, both Marshall and Morrell have recognized the need to identify and describe the various modes novelists utilize in the process of creating fiction. But their disparate lists raise several questions: (1) Which is the more appropriate label for the concept: writing modes, fiction-writing modes, delivery modes, or something else? (2) Are all of the terms listed by Marshall and Morrell appropriate for inclusion in a list of modes? (3) Are all the potential modes included in their lists?

Let's take the question of a label first. The term *delivery modes* has some merit, but in my mind it creates an image of big vans driven by people in brown shorts. So let's try another one. When I did a Google search using the keywords "writing modes," I found that the term is already used to describe four broad types of writing: descriptive, expository, narrative, and persuasive. I vaguely remember these terms from my school days, so in deference to

English teachers and their students, maybe we should leave writing modes to the classroom.

When I studied the Google search results for "writing modes," I saw that narrative writing refers to storytelling. Aha! Maybe we should label the modes as narrative modes or narrative-writing modes. Both have appeal, but the word *narrative* bothers me because it means different things to different people, especially writers.

Maybe Marshall has the right label, after all, with "fiction-writing modes." Fiction writing is consistent with the concept of narrative writing, and the term has little room for misunderstanding. Alternatively, "novel-writing modes" excludes short stories, and the modes encompass both forms of fiction. Until someone comes up with a better label, I'll use "fiction-writing modes."

Now, let's look at the second and third questions. Are all of the modes listed by Marshall and Morrell appropriate to include on the list? Could there be more? To answer that question, I combined both lists. Then I added more candidates: scene, sequel, stimulus, response, flashback, background, feelings/thoughts, narrative, description, action, summary, dialogue, exposition, transition, recollection, introspection, sensation, and emotion.

I eliminated *scene*, *sequel*, *stimulus*, and *response*, because I categorize them as structural components of plot:

- Macrostructure: beginning, middle, and ending
- Midlevel structure: scene and sequel
- Microstructure: stimulus and response

I deleted *flashback* from the mode list because I consider a flashback to be a scene within a sequel or, less appropriately, within another scene.

Background didn't make my list, either; it's essentially the backstory of a plot, and I view plot as having three temporal dimensions:

- Backstory: what happens before the beginning words of the written story
- Current story: what happens in the "now" of the story
- Future story: what happens, or could happen, after "The End"

Backstory, current story, and future story can each be revealed in numerous ways: dialogue, exposition, narration, recollection, or flashbacks.

Marshall's concept of *thinking/feeling* as a mode makes sense, but the term seemed cumbersome and incomplete. In its place I inserted introspection, recollection, emotion, and sensation.

Again, the term *narration* troubled me. Not only is it one of the four general writing modes, but it also encompasses everything a fiction writer produces. On the other hand, in a more narrow sense, *narration* is a specific type of writing where the narrator communicates directly to the reader. With this application in mind, I've retained narration as a fiction-writing mode.

Likewise, the term *description* in its broadest sense could be taken to include all fiction. What is dialogue but a description of conversation? Or, isn't action just a description of what is currently happening? But some writing clearly focuses on describing something specific and isn't easily categorized in another mode, so I kept *description* as a fiction-writing mode.

After combining the Marshall and Morrell lists, adding more candidates, winnowing the list, and then converting them to nouns ending in *-tion*, I arrived at the following list of fiction-writing modes: action, summarization, conversation, narration, description, exposition, transition, sensation, emotion, introspection, and recollection.

Join me now in exploring each fiction-writing mode and how each can work for you.

PART I

INTERIORITY

Four fiction-writing modes may be classified as *interiority*, as they reflect the inner workings of your character's mind: sensation, emotion, introspection, and recollection.

1

SENSATION

The fiction-writing mode that evokes the five senses (sight, hearing, touch, smell, and taste).

CHAPTER CONTENTS
Verbs of sensation
Adverbs
Adjectives
Onomatopoeia
Other word choices
Comparison
Symbolism
Intensity
Character emotion
Physical reaction
Relative power of senses
Intimacy of senses
The sixth sense
Choosing sensations

*S*ensation is the fiction-writing mode that enables a reader to see, hear, feel, smell, and taste the story's world, helping her experience fiction as if living it herself.

Sensation provides the vivid detail that brings action to life, creating verisimilitude. For example, the taste and smell of blood during a battle scene. Sensation can stimulate recollection, which may be helpful in communicating backstory. For example, the smell of perfume may trigger a character to recall fond memories of a lover.

Sensation can be a powerful tool for character development, especially regarding a character's emotional responses to particular stimuli. The sight of a puppy may generate feelings of happiness, while a spider's touch may engender revulsion or fear. Likewise, a character's reaction to sensations may provide a common thread for the development of one or more of a story's themes. For example, the recurring sound of distant drums may remind the reader of the presence of danger.

As a fiction writer, you have a variety of issues to address when conveying sensation: syntax (verbs of sensation, action verbs, adverbs, adjectives, onomatopoeia, and word choices); figures of speech (comparison and symbolism); emotional connections (intensity, character emotion, reader emotion, and physical reaction); and others (hierarchy of senses, sixth sense, and choice of sensation).

VERBS OF SENSATION

The basic verbs of sensation are *see, hear, feel, smell,* and *taste*. For any particular passage involving a character's perception through the senses, you face the choice of whether or not to utilize the applicable verb of sensation.

Here's an example using verbs of sensation (in italics):

> Dirk paused at the back door of the livery stable. He *smelled* a mixture of prairie hay and manure. He *could see* horse stalls to his right and rows of saddle racks to the left. He *heard* a horse whinny and stomp its hooves.

An alternative to using the verbs of sensation (once the viewpoint character is established) is simply to describe the sensation. For example,

> Dirk paused at the back door of the livery stable. The air reeked of prairie hay and manure. On his right stood horse stalls. To his left, rows of saddle racks. A horse whinnied and stomped its hooves.

Evan Marshall, in *The Marshall Plan for Getting Your Novel Published*, explains, "Though it's desirable to make use of your character's senses in your writing, it's rarely necessary to use the actual verbs of perception such as *saw*, *heard*, and *smelled*. Ironically, these words distance the reader from your viewpoint character because they remind the reader that he is not actually living the story through the character."[1]

ADVERBS

As a fiction-writing mode, sensation is vulnerable to the overuse of modifiers. Adverbs, especially those that end in *-ly*, tend to dilute the effectiveness of description. For example (adverbs in italics),

> A horse whinnied *shrilly* and stomped its hooves *nervously*.

Depending upon the context and objective, the adverbs *shrilly* and *nervously* may be unnecessary, even distracting. Here's the same example without the adverbs:

> A horse whinnied and stomped its hooves.

Omitting the adverbs presents leaner description that lets the reader fill in the blanks as to how the horse whinnied and stomped its feet. Sometimes an adverb adds just the right touch; sometimes it deadens the sensation. It's a case-by-case decision, depending on a host of variables, including context, pacing, and tone.

ADJECTIVES

Adjectives can provide interesting details that add realism, but adjectives can also dilute sensation. For example,

> Pungent smoke filled the air, and Frank coughed.

The adjective *pungent* provides detail, but it isn't necessary. Isn't all smoke pungent? Would the character cough if the smoke weren't pungent? Consider the sentence without it.

> Smoke filled the air, and Frank coughed.

Depending upon the context and objectives, omitting the adjectives creates leaner description that allows the reader to participate by filling in the blanks.

Adjectives can also create an unintended sense of restriction. For example,

> Frank coughed from the pungent smoke.

Was another type of smoke present? Did he cough at the pungent smoke but not at the acrid smoke or the putrid smoke? In many cases, a leaner description works best. For example,

Frank coughed from the smoke.

These examples illustrate another pitfall of writing sensation—describing it. Rather than trying to describe the sensation, you might better serve the reader by establishing a context so the reader feels the sensation using his own experience. For example,

Frank tossed an old tire on the bonfire. Black smoke billowed skyward. That smell mixed with the stench of scalded chicken feathers. Frank coughed and gagged.

ONOMATOPOEIA

Hiss, murmur, boom, whir, buzz, plop, meow, gurgle, bang, hiccup, and *slurp.* Say each word aloud and note how the sound mimics the object or action represented. These words are called *onomatopoeia.* Say the words again, louder, and observe the movement of your lips, mouth, and tongue and how they contribute to the sensation of making the sound.

Onomatopoeia provides an opportunity to suggest sound and action with a single word. The use of such words adds richness to the depiction of sensation and contributes to making description feel real. Which of the following sentences provides the more effective description of sensation?

A fan turned noisily overhead.
A fan whirred overhead.
A fan creaked overhead.

See how the verbs *whir* and *creaked* suggest both motion and sound?

Onomatopoeic words may function as nouns or verbs. The duck *quacked*. The duck's *quack* echoed across the valley.

OTHER WORD CHOICES

Fortunately (even beyond verbs of sensation, action verbs, adjectives, adverbs, and onomatopoeia) a universe of words is available to portray sensation. The choice of one word over another can make a difference in effectively conveying sensation. For example, does a lover "touch" or does he "caress"? Should a smell be described as an "aroma"? A "scent"? An "odor"? A "stench"?

Does the word generate a positive or negative connotation? How does a change of words alter the emotional response? Which emotions are stimulated by each word choice? Sometimes, the differences are subtle; sometimes, they're substantial. Your job is to pick the word that best accomplishes the desired sensory effect.

COMPARISON

Stating what something smells, tastes, or feels like may be effective, but what if the reader is unlikely to recognize the sensation?[2] For example,

> Archie hesitated. The air reeked of rotten eggs.

Today, few of us raise chickens. Even people raised on a farm are unlikely to have smelled a rotten egg. Not too long ago, the smell of sulfur reminded many of rotten eggs. Readers today are more likely to recall the smell of sulfur from a high-school chemistry lab or a geyser in Yellowstone National Park.

A comparison to a familiar sensation may be helpful when attempting to communicate a sensation that the reader may not recognize.[3] Similes and metaphors may be applicable. For example,

> The martini tasted like a combination of kerosene and olive oil.

Sometimes a sensation may be best described through contrast.

> The detective wet his finger, dipped it into the powder, and tasted it. It was not salty, but it was also not sweet.

Comparisons may best be taken from the milieu the character inhabits. For instance, a cowboy would naturally compare with a horse, but a man who lives in Manhattan would not be likely to do so.

Sometimes an effective description is stating what something *doesn't* taste like.

> Not bad, but it certainly wasn't Mom's apple pie.

SYMBOLISM

Sometimes sensation can take on a greater meaning: something seemingly insignificant can call attention to the bigger picture. The subtle use of symbols can be an effective means of reinforcing themes. For example, if you make the smell of food a recurring sensation in your story, its frequency, intensity, and nature may be representing a theme such as family cohesion and contentment.

The taste of bourbon could symbolize the struggles of a hard-bitten detective. A color or colors might mirror or contrast with a theme. For example, lush green could signify bounty or health, while pea-soup green may suggest decay or illness.

INTENSITY

Sensation has a range of intensities, from overwhelming to absence. Think of movies where action scenes rumble so loudly they can shake popcorn out of its box. But then the aftermath may be marked by softness or silence. In some situations you may want to project intensity. Other circumstances warrant subtle sensation or even the absence of sensation.[4]

Here's an example of intensity from *The Brute*.

> The tent snapped from side to side, then collapsed. The shrieking wind pummeled Fort through the thin nylon canvas. As the flattened tent flipped over, it hurled him up and then dropped him to the ground, pounding the wind out of him. He heard Billy scream. Before Fort could reach for him, the tent began to roll, and they tumbled helplessly inside it.
>
> Fort's stomach ached as the tent fabric plastered against his face, suffocating him. Gasping and clawing at the canvas, he could feel himself being propelled upward with incredible speed. He tried to scream, but no sound came. He tried to reach out to find Billy, but his arms wouldn't move. He plunged downward, then up, rolling and spinning over and over again.

This action sequence is immediately followed by a segment with less intense sensation.

Then everything slowed. He could still hear the powerful, rushing roar, but it seemed farther away. The tent fabric loosened its clinging hold on his face and body, and he could breathe again. The canvas fluttered and flapped. He stretched his arms and legs, feeling weightless, like an astronaut floating freely in a space capsule. For a split second, time and motion stopped—a carefree sensation, so different from the horror of moments earlier.

Then the sensation returns to higher intensity.

In an instant, the sensation of weightlessness evaporated. He was falling. His stomach seemed to hang in his mouth...

Unrelenting high intensity can exhaust the reader, dulling the impact of the story. Conversely, sustained subtlety or the absence of sensation can fail to stimulate the reader, or worse, bore her. Varying the level of intensity of sensation provides the reader with a richer, more enjoyable experience.

CHARACTER EMOTION

Sensation can create emotion within a character, and that emotion may be used to channel the story in different directions. A character's attitude toward a sensation may reveal character.

Jennifer approached the football players. They reeked of sweat, and her pulse quickened.

Emotion may be used to transition into backstory.

> Horace studied his ink-stained fingers and was reminded of the crude tattoo he had acquired in prison. So many wasted years. So many disappointments.

Emotion may hint at a theme or help establish tone.

> Rita smelled chocolate and smiled. Life always seemed better with chocolate.

Emotions (such as fear, curiosity, frustration, anger, and lust) may advance plot by propelling the character into action.

> The air hung heavy with the smell of rotting flesh. Zombies were close. Ralph reached for his pistol.

PHYSICAL REACTION

Often the best way to communicate sensation is to portray the character's reaction to it.[5] Instead of describing a sensation or in addition to describing it, put more emphasis on character *reaction*. What sensations would make your character's mouth water? (The smell of buttered lobster.) What would make her skin crawl? (Contact with a snake.) What sensations would make her gag? Jump? Cough? Hold her nose?

As we'll discuss in the chapter about action, in real life and in fiction, stimulus precedes response. But according to Evan Marshall, "To show a character's reaction to something shocking, break the action/result rule and show the reaction before describing what is being reacted to." This may seem backward, but

"A tiny moment of suspense is created between the horrified reaction and the description of what's being seen."[6]

Here's an example of sensation followed by reaction (stimulus, then response):

A tarantula crawled up Laurie's arm. She screamed.

Here's an example of response *preceding* stimulus:

Laurie screamed. A tarantula had crawled up her arm.

RELATIVE POWER OF SENSES

Depending on the situation, some senses are more powerful than others. The sense of smell may be the most enduring of the five senses (I can vividly recall the aroma of my grandmother's fresh rye bread, decades ago). Earlier in man's history, a robust sense of smell—and the memory to catalog them—often meant the difference between life and death in the hunt for prey amidst predators. The fact that your reader's olfactory memory is laden with treasures is reason enough to take full advantage of it. If smell truly is the most profound and longest-lasting of the physical senses, you should tap into it often to engage your readers more fully.[7]

Closely related to smell is the sense of taste. If you hold your nose and try to taste something, you can taste almost nothing. Taste may be the most reliable of the senses. Think of cinnamon, pepper, sugar, and salt. What something tastes like can be synonymous with what it is; its essence.

On the other hand, some senses can be misleading. Is that the smell of perfume or rotten fruit? You may not be aware that whether you touch something hot or something cold, your nervous system may react but does not immediately sense the difference. Try it the next time you turn on your shower: for a moment, you can't tell whether the water is too cold or too hot.

INTIMACY OF SENSES

According to Todd A. Stone in his *Novelist's Boot Camp*, some senses are more intimate than others. He outlines a hierarchy of senses, ranging from least intimate to most intimate: sight, sound, touch, smell, and taste. Stone encourages writers to build a connection between the reader and the story by using the more-intimate senses to make descriptions emotionally powerful.[8]

To get a feel for the telescoping effect of intimacy in sensation, try this exercise. Imagine...

- Seeing a coffeepot
- Hearing coffee dripping into the pot
- Touching the hot pot
- Smelling the aroma
- Tasting the fresh brew

THE SIXTH SENSE

You aren't limited to sight, hearing, touch, smell, and taste. With a sixth sense, the character can gain information without the aid of recognized physical senses. A sixth sense may be presented in the form of extrasensory perception (ESP), telepathy, clairaudience, clairvoyance, or what I call the transtemporal functions of precognition or retrocognition. These concepts may be more casually represented as instinct, hunch, or intuition—or merely "sensing" something may be about to happen, or having a "bad feeling" about somebody or someplace. A sixth sense implies the acquisition of information by means external to human logic.[9]

CHOOSING SENSATIONS

If you were a carpenter, you wouldn't build a cabinet using just one tool. You might use a saw, and you would probably also use hammers, chisels, planes, and routers. Each performs a unique and necessary function. In writing, each sense provides unique opportunities to deepen the reader's experience, so why not use them all? This may seem obvious, but the popularity of movies and television can lead to a cinematic treatment of written fiction, where sight and sound are the only sensations represented.

Limiting portrayal of sensation to sight may also mean that the writer is overusing the least intimate of the sensations and failing to make effective use of more intimate sensations.

One of the advantages written fiction has over other forms of fiction (such as movies, plays, and television) is the ability to employ all the senses, including touch, taste, and smell. Choice of sensation doesn't necessarily mean selecting just one sensation. Real life engages more than one sensation at a time. Why shouldn't written fiction?

TAKEAWAYS

1. Sensation may be a powerful tool in developing plot, character, setting, and theme.
2. The basic verbs of sensation are *see, hear, feel, smell*, and *taste*.
3. Adverbs, especially those ending in *-ly*, may dilute the effectiveness of the description of sensation.

4. Choose adjectives carefully when using them to describe sensation, to avoid redundancy and inappropriate restriction.
5. Onomatopoeia provides an opportunity to suggest both sight and sound with a single word.
6. Word choice may be especially important in portraying sensation.
7. Comparison and contrast may be an effective means of communicating sensation.
8. Sensation may be an effective means of creating symbolism.
9. Sensation has a range of intensity from overwhelming to absent.
10. Link sensation to emotion for extra effectiveness.
11. A character's physical reaction may be one of the best ways to convey sensation.
12. A hierarchy of sensations shows that sensations vary in intimacy.
13. With a sixth sense, characters may gain information without the aid of the recognized physical senses.
14. Choice of sensation is an opportunity to add depth to fiction.

In real life and in fiction, sensation often accompanies emotion. The next chapter explores the mode that evokes emotions.

2

EMOTION

The fiction-writing mode that relates how a character feels.

CHAPTER CONTENTS
Techniques for conveying emotion
Context
Selection of technique
Repetition
Narrative distance
Clichés
Setting
Props
Choice of emotion
Range of emotion
Intensity
Appropriateness
Emotional complexity
Emotional consistency
Sacrifice
Emotional journey

What would you guess is the number-one reason people read fiction? It's to have an emotional experience: to be amused, amazed, enchanted, saddened, thrilled, even terrified.[1] The goal of writers, then, is to stimulate the reader's emotion. The writer's primary means of generating reader reaction is to portray emotion in the story's characters. *Emotion* is the fiction-writing mode used to convey a character's feelings.

Emotion may be communicated with any of eight techniques: narration, exposition, conversation, introspection, recollection, reaction, action, and abstention.

NARRATION

The easiest means of adding emotion to a story is for the narrator to state or label the character's emotion. For example (emotion in italics),

> As Harry approached the garage, he felt a growing sense of *concern.*

EXPOSITION

One step beyond simply stating an emotion is to explain it or tell about it—to provide additional information, as in exposition. For example (exposition in italics),

> Harry approached the garage. He felt a growing sense of concern, *because if Maugans got his way, innocent people could get hurt or killed.*

CONVERSATION

Emotion may be conveyed through dialogue. For example,

> As Harry approached the garage, he grabbed Billy by the shoulder. *"I'm worried that if Maugans gets his way, innocent people could get hurt—or killed."*

INTROSPECTION

Emotion may be conveyed through a character's thoughts. For example (thinking verb in italics),

> As Harry approached the garage, he *realized* that if Maugans got his way, innocent people could get hurt or killed.

RECOLLECTION

A character recalling something may stimulate emotion. For example (verb of recollection in italics),

> As Harry approached the garage, he *remembered* that Maugans had beaten the town drunk to death.

REACTION

In real life, people react physically to emotion. Bodily reactions to emotion range from subtle to extreme: goosebumps, blushing, sweating, hair standing on end, an increased heart rate, laughing uncontrollably or sobbing, an upset stomach, shaking, jangled nerves, vomiting, and even loss of bladder or bowel control. For example (bodily reaction in italics),

As Harry approached the garage, *his heart pounded, and his insides tightened.*

ACTION

Emotion may be portrayed through physical action.[2] Action that expresses emotion may range from subtle to pronounced. Here's an example of subtle action (in italics).

As Harry approached the house, *he clenched his fist.*

Here's an example of pronounced action (in italics).

Harry approached the house, *drew his pistol, and kicked the door open.*

ABSTENTION

Sometimes, leaving emotion out of a passage may be the most effective approach to stimulating a reader's emotions. In this technique, the writer creates a situation that should stimulate emotion but doesn't depict the character's response, leaving the reader to fill in the reaction himself. The character abstains from showing emotion. Orson Scott Card explains it this way: "If your characters cry, your readers won't have to; if your characters have good reason to cry and don't, your readers will do that weeping."[3]

For example,

Cisco sat quietly at the poker table as the town mayor described how Bart had brutally raped the schoolteacher and left her in a ditch.

Cisco folded his hand and laid his cards face down. He shoved his chair back from the table and headed for the door.

In this example the character doesn't demonstrate emotion. His action is incidental. The reader doesn't yet know the character's emotion. (He may step outside to vomit, or he may be enraged to violence.)

Withholding emotion doesn't fit every situation, but in the appropriate circumstances, it can be powerful.

Review the examples above and note that they are arranged roughly in order of effectiveness in conveying emotion. Narration and exposition are forms of telling rather than showing and are thus the least powerful. Conversation, introspection, reaction, and action show emotion and are thus more effective. In some situations, abstention from an emotional response may be the most effective technique.

OTHER ISSUES

In addition to using the eight basic techniques of conveying emotion, the author faces other issues related to portraying emotion: context, selection of technique, repetition, narrative distance, clichés, setting, props, choice of emotion, range of emotion, intensity, appropriateness, emotional complexity, emotional consistency, sacrifice, and emotional journey.

CONTEXT

Emotions shouldn't pop up without warning; they require development. Successful portrayal of emotion depends on context, which requires a buildup to make emotions feel genuine. Emotion is an effect, so it requires a stimulus.[4] The writer needs to show the cause that makes a character experience the emotion, so the reader can share it.

For example, before showing Cisco's concern or anger, establish that Bart is a murdering, thieving, raping marauder. Provide context so the reader can believe Cisco's emotion when it surfaces.

SELECTION OF TECHNIQUE

Just because a writer's emotion-stimulating toolbox contains lots of tools doesn't mean she should use all of them for every task. For one thing, the effect could be redundant, even melodramatic. Consider the following:

> Hanna felt her anger grow. Darin had cheated. Her heart pounded, and she clenched her fist. "Damn you." Hanna slapped Darin's face.

In writing, less is often more. Selecting the single best technique for a particular situation may be more effective than combining many of them. Here's an example using just two, stating emotion and dialogue.

> Hanna felt her anger grow. "Damn you, Darin."

Here's an example using just one (action).

> Hanna slapped Darin's face.

Depending upon the circumstances and the writer's objectives, any one or any combination of the seven techniques for conveying emotion may be right for a particular task.

REPETITION

Portraying a character's emotion once may add to that character's development, but too much repetition of that emotion may dilute its effect. Repetition can also make the writing melodramatic, even farcical.[5] Unless melodrama or farce is the intended effect, repetition of the emotion should be avoided. Here's an example of using repetition to create a melodramatic or farcical effect.

> Sundance glanced at his cards and decided to fold. Before he could lay his hand down, the saloon doors swung open. In strode Hank, his steps thundering on the pine floor. A broom leaning against the bar fell, its handle landing at Hank's feet. He tumbled to the floor face-first, and the bar patrons erupted in laughter.
>
> Hank's face turned dark red. He clutched a chair and staggered to his feet, but his left boot caught a spittoon and tipped it over, splashing tobacco juice across his pants. Someone howled hysterically, and the bar again echoed with laughter.

NARRATIVE DISTANCE

Written fiction always has a narrator.[6] That narrator may be a character or an identified storyteller ("I'm an old man now, but let me tell you about the time..."). Or, the narrator may be an unnamed persona that communicates the story, either obtrusively ("Once upon a time...") or so unobtrusively that the story appears to have no narrator at all (as is the case with the majority of popular fiction told in the third person).

Whether the narration is obtrusive or unobtrusive, the narrator may tell the story from a point of view that ranges from very distant to so close that the narrator seems to occupy a character's mind.

Emotion may be conveyed through distant narration, but it becomes more effective the closer the narration approaches intimacy with the point-of-view character. Here's an example of emotion conveyed with substantial distance:

> Mark recalled that tender yet terrifying moment of his first kiss.

Here's an example of conveying emotion up close:

> Mark's heart pounded as he brushed back her hair. Terrified that she would push him away, he leaned close and kissed her.

CLICHÉS

Some phrases and expressions intended to convey emotion have been used so frequently that they no longer stimulate feelings. Here are examples:

- Mad as a hornet
- Happy as a clam
- Green with envy
- Butterflies in stomach

We have all heard and likely used clichés, so they tend to surface in our minds when writing. The use of clichés in a first draft (where the primary objective is to get the story in written form as quickly as possible) is understandable, but they should be replaced during revision. Rather than resorting to clichés, use one of the eight techniques to convey emotion: narration, exposition, conversation, introspection, recollection, reaction, action, and abstention.

SETTING

Stories have a physical world, or *milieu,* that includes history, culture, and society. The setting of a story can create a backdrop to suggest emotion. Here's an example of using setting to suggest a mood or to enhance it.

Russo stepped into the ditch and approached the body lying face down. Thunder rumbled in the distance.

PROPS

Props may be used to demonstrate emotion. Here's an example of using a prop to suggest or reinforce emotion.

Despite his anger, Cagney realized he was about to break the law. He pulled the tin star off his shirt and slipped it into his pocket.

CHOICE OF EMOTION

You have the choice of countless emotions: repulsion, terror, ecstasy, passion, love, hate, desire, fear, anger, disgust, spite, forgiveness, annoyance, peevishness.

With so many alternatives, which emotions should you choose? That depends on the context of the story and your objectives. Any emotion can be portrayed in fiction, and doubtless, every conceivable emotion probably has been. Your novel will likely include a wide range of emotions, reflecting various situations within the plot. Genre often determines which emotions dominate a particular story. Fear would likely pervade a horror story. Yearning and passion might rule in a love story.

One emotion stands above all others as the most useful in fiction: frustration.[7] The essence of a plot is a character repeatedly attempting but often failing to achieve a series of objectives until the climax, where the character overcomes all resistance and succeeds. The emotional byproduct of falling short of an objective is frustration.

In fiction, the default emotion is frustration. When in doubt about which emotion to portray, try frustration. If the story's plot doesn't frustrate the character, rework the plot so it does.

RANGE OF EMOTION

During the story's ebb and flow, a character should experience a variety of emotions appropriate to the circumstances. A range of emotions gives characters depth and complexity. For example, here's a passage from the first chapter of *The Brute*.

> The thought of the younger Scouts made his forehead throb. He had promised he would control his temper, but that morning, at the Newton Ranch headquarters, he had lost his cool and slugged one of his little brothers. Fort remembered the flash of anger and disappointment in his father's eyes.

> To make matters worse, he had socked his little brother in front of Tana Newton, the ranch owner's niece. His face flushed in spite of the cool night air, and he wiped beads of

sweat from his forehead. He pictured Tana on her horse at the ranch house—white cowboy hat over her long brown hair, brown eyes sparkling, and a teasing smile on her friendly face.

Just thinking about her made his insides ache. Their fingers had touched momentarily, and electricity had coursed through him. He couldn't wait to see her again, to get to know her, to touch her, to...

Now let's analyze the passage, noting the emotions and the techniques used to convey them (in parentheses).

The thought of the younger Scouts made his forehead throb (anxiety—bodily reaction). He had promised he would control his temper, but that morning, at the Newton Ranch headquarters, he had lost his cool and slugged one of his little brothers (anger—recollection). Fort remembered the flash of anger and disappointment in his father's eyes (shame—recollection).

To make matters worse, he had socked his little brother in front of Tana Newton, the ranch owner's niece (embarrassment—recollection). His face flushed in spite of the cool night air, and he wiped beads of sweat from his forehead (embarrassment—bodily reaction). He pictured Tana on her horse at the ranch house—white cowboy hat over her long brown hair, brown eyes sparkling, and a teasing smile on her friendly face (longing—recollection).

Just thinking about her made his insides ache (longing—bodily reaction). Their fingers had touched momentarily, and electricity had coursed through him (sexual excitement

—bodily reaction). He couldn't wait to see her again, to get to know her, to touch her, to... (lust—introspection).

INTENSITY

Intensity can range from subtle to extreme, even within the context of a single emotion or a set of related emotions. For example, mild annoyance to uncontrollable rage, amusement to hysterical laughter, or barely noticeable twinge to unbearable pain.

Intensity of emotion should rise and fall with the ebb and flow of the story, rising substantially at scene climaxes and then receding in sequels, rising tremendously at the story's climax, then ebbing in the story's denouement.

APPROPRIATENESS

According to an old adage, writers should "open a vein" and let the emotion flow. But you don't want too much of a good thing. The opposite of the unemotional portrayal of characters is the melodramatic or sentimental portrayal of characters.

The words *melodramatic* and *sentimental* can mean different things to different people, but dictionary definitions include *exaggerated, overdramatic, excessive,* and *indulgent.* The common ground refers not so much to intensity as to appropriateness within context.

Here's an example of melodramatic portrayal of emotion.

> Elizabeth flinched. "Oh, no!" she screamed in horror. The nail on her left pinky had chipped. Her lips quivered. She felt tears well up in her eyes. She moaned in agony, then grabbed a tissue as she began to sob. Doubling over, she slumped to the floor, then pounded the carpet with her fists.

In the world of fiction, there may be a situation where this portrayal of emotion would be appropriate (for example, if the character had anticipated winning a million dollars at an international manicure contest). Otherwise, it's just melodramatic.

Portrayal of emotion doesn't have to be as extreme as in the example above to be melodramatic. Any portrayal of emotion that exceeds the emotion appropriate to the situation risks distracting or annoying the reader.

EMOTIONAL COMPLEXITY

According to Ann Hood, "Perhaps the most important thing to remember when searching for emotional honesty is that emotion is not one-dimensional. Emotions are complex and often mixed together. Think of a bride on her wedding day. It would be too easy and too flat to describe her as simply happy. Instead, she is excited, apprehensive, worried, fearful, anxious, joyful, smug—so many emotions!"[8]

In *Writer's Digest*, August 2004, Nancy Kress echoes this thought: "Frustration isn't a 'pure' emotion." It can come mixed with many others, including anger, hurt, fear, self-blame, resignation, bitterness, and more.[9]

Sometimes these emotions feed off one another. Here's an example of mixed emotions (emotions in parentheses and italics).

> Garrett paused at the door. If he stepped into the street and faced Billy, he might be able to stop Billy from hurting innocent people (*hopeful determination*). But Garrett also realized that his own chances of surviving the fight were slim. Billy was fast with a six-shooter—very fast (*fear*).

EMOTIONAL CONSISTENCY

Characters are a representation of humans, and that means they are both consistent *and* inconsistent in their emotions. Ann Hood reminds writers that Aristotle observed that a character should be "consistently inconsistent," which does not mean characters jump from emotion to emotion recklessly, but rather that they move believably from one emotion to the next.[10]

A well-developed character might experience a range of emotions in one situation. During the commission of a bank robbery, a character might experience terror, courage, and disbelief, then experience an entirely different set of emotions during the next situation. As police investigate the robbery, for example, the same character might experience shock, guilt, shame, pride, or several of these emotions at once.

SACRIFICE

According to Orson Scott Card, in *Characters and Viewpoint*, "Pain or grief also increase a reader's intensity in proportion to a character's degree of choice. Self-chosen suffering for the sake of a greater good—sacrifice, in other words—is far more intense than pain alone."[11]

Here's an example.

> Garrett paused at the door. If he faced Billy, he might be able to stop Billy from hurting innocent people. But Garrett also realized that his chances of surviving the fight were slim. Billy was fast with a six-shooter—very fast. Besides, thought Garrett, this really wasn't his fight—he could just ride out of town and never return.

Garrett took a deep breath, then stepped into the street.

EMOTIONAL JOURNEY

Coincident with a story's physical journey (*external plot*) is the character's emotional journey (*internal plot*), which may appear as a rollercoaster of feelings that, in turn, provide the character with internal growth, such as maturity or wisdom.

The story as a whole is an emotional journey. Viewing story structure in three acts, the character begins the story in a state of equilibrium. The essence of a beginning is an incident that upsets the equilibrium and turns the character's emotional world upside down. A series of emotion-packed scenes and sequels comprise the middle of the story as action and emotion rise to the inevitable climax, where unbearable emotion explodes in either success or failure. The ending shows the world in a new state of equilibrium, in which the character moves forward with a greater sense of peace.

A fully developed scene has an internal plot:

- The character (reluctantly, confidently, desperately, fearfully) sets out to achieve his objective.
- Along the way he encounters an obstacle that frustrates his intentions.
- He may encounter several obstacles that ratchet his frustration to increasingly tense levels.
- At the scene's climax, his frustration reaches a breaking point, and then he either succeeds or fails to achieve his objective.[12]

A fully developed sequel also includes an emotional journey:

- A sequel may begin with the character teeming with emotion, ranging from devastation to exhilaration.
- After a brief respite to let the emotion subside, he reviews the events that brought him to his present situation.
- He devises alternative actions for moving forward.
- After weighing the merits and pitfalls of each, he selects one.
- With renewed resolve and confidence, he is ready to proceed into the next scene.[13]

TAKEAWAYS

1. Emotion may be conveyed with any of eight techniques: narration, exposition, conversation, introspection, recollection, reaction, action, and abstention.
2. Emotion requires some indication of its cause.
3. Selecting the best technique for presenting an emotion may be more effective than combining techniques.
4. Repetition may reinforce emotion, but too much repetition may dilute its effect, possibly even creating melodrama.
5. Emotion may be conveyed through distant narration, but it becomes more effective the closer narration approaches intimacy with the point-of-view character.
6. Clichés are phrases or expressions that have been used so frequently they no longer stimulate emotion.
7. Setting may be used to help generate or reinforce emotion.
8. Props may be used to demonstrate emotion.
9. Although a story should include many emotions, the most important emotion in a story is usually frustration.

10. During the ebb and flow of a story, a character should experience a variety of emotions.
11. Intensity may range from subtle to extreme, and should rise and fall with the flow of the story.
12. Inappropriately excessive emotion may lead to melodramatic or sentimental portrayal of characters.
13. Emotions are complex and often are mixed together.
14. Emotional consistency means that a character moves believably from one emotion to the next.
15. Self-chosen suffering for the sake of a greater good is more intense than pain alone.
16. The story as a whole, as well as its component scenes and sequels, should include an emotional journey.

We've explored sensation and emotion. In the next chapter let's delve into a character's thinking.

3

INTROSPECTION

The fiction-writing mode that shares a character's thinking.

CHAPTER CONTENTS
Characterization
Stimulus-internalization-response
Setting
Theme
Formatting
Attributions
Paragraphs
Verbs of thought
Tense
Person
Narrative distance
Direct introspection
Indirect introspection
Direct introspection vs. indirect introspection
Epiphany

Can you name the biggest advantage written fiction has over other forms of storytelling, such as poetry, plays, television, and movies? Written fiction most effectively allows the audience to experience what is going through a character's mind.

Introspection is the fiction-writing mode used to convey a character's thoughts. As a means of developing character, plot, setting, and theme, introspection is potentially one of the most powerful fiction-writing modes.

CHARACTERIZATION

A reader can learn a lot about a character by what he says, but a character may also say things he doesn't believe. He may choose not to say everything he is thinking, and that may allow the reader to learn a lot about that character, too—maybe more than if his thoughts match his words. Introspection is a window into the character's mind and heart.

In the broadest sense, *characterization* includes the character's background, attitudes, and beliefs. *What* a character thinks about—what's important to her—helps define her. *How* a character thinks (her method of reasoning) reveals something about that character, too.[1]

As with dialogue, introspection can reflect regional or ethnic dialect and provide a sense of the character's background. How the character views his environment and his attitude toward it helps establish his worldview.

Consistent repetition throughout the story of what and how the character thinks and how she solves problems helps confirm who the character is. For example, an analytical character may solve her problems by planning an elaborate scheme. A physical, reactive person might dismiss advance planning in favor of swift action.

Introspection may also validate character change by demonstrating that the character's attitude is different after the change.[2] For example, a character bent on revenge may change his attitude after experiencing bloody violence, and his thinking could change accordingly, confirming that the change is heartfelt and likely permanent.

PLOT

Introspection may occur anywhere in a story, from action scenes to quiet reflection. The essence of a scene is the character attempting to reach a goal. For that action to be believable, the reader needs to understand the character's motivation. And what better means of understanding a character's reason for action than through his own thoughts?

The smallest structural component of plot is cause and effect.[3] Action leads to reaction, but every stimulus-response sequence requires communication between body and mind. Think of the simplest of medical procedures, when the doctor taps the patient's leg to test reflexes. The stimulus generates a signal to the nervous system, which in turn generates a knee-jerk reaction.

Except in the most reflexive reactions, stimulus is followed by mental processing, or *internalization*. Often a character's reaction is immediate and without apparent thought. But in other situations, even in the heat of battle, the character can and should think before acting. Whether or not portrayed, this internalization occurs every time. In simple situations and in those that are complicated, the sequence is *stimulus-internalization-response*.[4]

Introspection may also be used to increase tension. For example, a character's thoughts may conflict with his or her actions or dialogue, indicating that the character is lying or delusional.

A *scene* is a passage of writing in which the character attempts to achieve a goal. A *sequel* is a passage of writing in which a character reflects on the outcome of a scene. While scenes are mainly physical and external to the character, sequels are mostly in the head. As outlined by Jack M. Bickham in *Scene & Structure*, a sequel consists of the following phases: emotion, thought (including review, analysis, and planning), and decision.[5] Each phase of a sequel provides ample opportunity for the use of introspection.

SETTING

What a character thinks about the world around him adds depth to the story. Here's an example (introspection in italics).

> Fort breathed in the fresh aroma of rain-washed prairie. Goosebumps prickled his arms as he absorbed the panoramic view before him. *In his mind he could picture the vast buffalo herds that once covered the land. For a moment he imagined that he was an Indian brave watching a wagon train of pioneers crossing the prairie.*

Here's another example.

> Big chunks of stone littered the cavern floor. Bodie glanced at the ceiling. *A cave-in had occurred here. He wondered how far under the surface he was now, and how many thousands of tons of rock were above him. What if...? He imagined a mountain of rock crushing his body into a bloody pile of goo buried forever.* A chill ran deep through his bones. He groaned.

THEME

Introspection provides an opportunity to engage the reader deeply. While both the external and internal plots may be entertaining, the story resonates at long-lasting levels if its theme helps the reader see the world through different eyes. Introspection can widen the scope of the story, adding complexity and depth. Here's an example.

> At first, life with the Duncans had been pretty good, and Bodie had felt as if he was part of a family. But these last few years, he thought the Duncans would drive him crazy, always nagging him to clean up his room or do chores around the house. I'm nearly grown up, he reasoned, but they're always wanting to know where I'm going, who I'm hanging around with, and when I'll be back home. They're always telling me what to do and what not to do.
>
> They just don't understand me and what I've been through, thought Bodie. Not that they hadn't kept trying. He would give them credit for that. They even offered to adopt me, he recalled. What a pair of saps.
>
> He wondered if the Duncans even missed him. They're probably relieved that I'm finally out of their lives, hoping they'll never see me again. Anyway, they're better off without me.

Theme is the "why" of a story and, as the example above shows, introspection can be used to communicate the character's perspective about issues touched upon throughout the story.

Effective use of a character's thoughts in fiction requires a thorough understanding of the mechanics of introspection, which include formatting, attributions, paragraph treatment, verbs of thought, tense, person, narrative distance, direct introspection, indirect introspection, and epiphany.

FORMATTING

Over the years, various formats have been used to delineate introspection. In the past, some writers used quotation marks to identify a character's thoughts. This practice caused confusion since quotation marks are the accepted means of identifying dialogue.

Introspection has also been denoted with italics, but placing introspection in italics is a glaring reminder that an author is at work. The publishing industry's stylebook, *The Chicago Manual of Style*, gives readers two choices for presenting "unspoken discourse," and neither is italics.

Use plain type for introspection.

ATTRIBUTIONS

Just as dialogue can be tagged to identify the speaker, introspection may be attributed to making clear who is doing the thinking. An example of introspection *with* a tag (attribution in italics):

> Maybe Bonnie will listen to reason before someone gets hurt, *thought Clyde.*

Here's an example of introspection *without* an attribution:

> Maybe Bonnie will listen to reason before someone gets hurt.

When writing from a single point of view, attribution isn't usually necessary because the reader already understands who is doing the thinking.[6] Then again, sometimes a passage doesn't flow smoothly without a tag to provide rhythm and pace.

One final thought regarding attribution for introspection: unless the character is telepathic, avoid tags like *he thought to himself*. Who else would the character be thinking to?[7]

PARAGRAPHS

Introspection may be embedded within a paragraph that also includes action, dialogue, or some other fiction-writing mode, but sometimes introspection warrants its own paragraph. Here's an example of introspection embedded within a paragraph (introspection in italics).

> A copper-colored, wormlike creature wriggled across the floor. Bodie froze. The creepy, three-inch bug's tiny legs blurred with motion as it skittered toward a crack in the cave wall. *A centipede or a millipede, thought Bodie, wondering how to tell the difference.*

Here's an example of introspection with its own paragraph.

> For a moment Bodie thought it might be interesting to learn more about geology. Then he caught himself and smiled. He knew what the adults were trying to do. The big idea behind this trip was to take a bunch of guys out in the woods and let them experience nature—to open their eyes to the world and to encourage each of them to turn his life around before it was too late. Right, thought Bodie. Like these losers are going to turn into regular library patrons.

The adults were chumps, but he would play along for the weekend.

VERBS OF THOUGHT

Verbs of thought may be used in attribution tags or within the introspection itself. Examples of thinking verbs include: *think, hope, wonder, pray, reason, realize, decide.* For example,

> Hercule thought he...
> ..., hoped Elizabeth.
> Ike wondered if...

These verbs have the advantage of being nearly as unobtrusive as the dialogue attribution *said*. There are, of course, many synonyms for these verbs, but other verbs of thought (such as *surmised* or *ruminated*) may distract, slow down, or annoy the reader.

TENSE

A character's thoughts may be narrated in past tense, present tense, future tense, or any of their variations (such as past perfect tense). Most stories (and their introspection) are written in past tense or present tense. Examples of introspection in present tense include:

> I think the cheese stinks.
> Darcy thinks he knows Elizabeth.

Examples in past tense.

> I thought the cheese stank.
> Darcy thought he knew Elizabeth.

He had thought of marrying her.

PERSON

Introspection may be written in any of three grammatical persons: first person, second person, or third person. For example,

I thought Ahab was insane.
You thought Ahab was insane.
Ishmael thought Ahab was insane.

The vast majority of introspection is written in either first person or third person.

NARRATIVE DISTANCE

Narrative distance ranges from distant (observing from the outside) to intimate (perceiving the world through the character's mind and senses). Here's an example of *first-person distant* introspection (introspection in italics).

Many years ago, when I was a young man, *I decided to pack a bag and leave home.*

Here's an example of *first-person intimate* introspection.

I grabbed my bag and stuffed in a clean shirt. *Realizing I wouldn't be back, I added socks, underwear, and my best pair of jeans.*

Here's an example of *third-person distant* introspection.

> A young man named Rudolfo *decided to pack a bag and leave home.*

Here's an example of *third-person intimate* introspection.

> Rudolfo grabbed his bag and stuffed in a clean shirt. *Realizing he wouldn't be back,* he added socks, underwear, and his best pair of jeans.

Introspection in the first person leaves little doubt about whose thoughts are being conveyed, so attribution tags are unlikely to be necessary.

When introspection is in the third person, the more distant the narrator is from the character, the more necessary attribution tags and thought verbs are to designate the passages as thoughts and clarify who is doing the thinking.

Introspection in the intimate third person is told from the viewpoint of the character's mind, so who is doing the thinking is usually apparent without attributions.

DIRECT INTROSPECTION

Direct introspection uses the character's exact words, while *indirect introspection* summarizes or paraphrases the thinker's words.[8]

Direct introspection conveys the character's exact words in first person, present tense.[9] For example,

> I hope Bonnie will listen to reason before someone gets hurt.

Although direct introspection is in the first person, the personal pronoun *I* need not appear in the introspection. For example,

> Maybe Bonnie will listen to reason before someone gets hurt.

Direct introspection may be expressed with or without tags to identify the thinker. For example (attribution tag in italics),

> Maybe Bonnie will listen to reason before someone gets hurt, *thought Clyde.*

Direct introspection has clear strengths:

- The first person gives the narration a sense of intimacy.
- Present tense gives the narration a sense of immediacy.
- Using the thinker's exact words creates both intimacy and immediacy.

INDIRECT INTROSPECTION

While *direct introspection* uses the character's exact words, *indirect introspection* summarizes or paraphrases the thinker's words.[10]

Here's an example of *first-person* indirect introspection.

> I hoped Bonnie would listen to reason.

Here's an example of *third-person* indirect introspection.

> Clyde hoped Bonnie would listen to reason.

Indirect introspection has clear advantages: it summarizes thinking, compressing it into fewer words, requiring less space and less time to read. But indirect narration also has distinct disadvantages (which mirror the advantages of direct introspection).

- Third person may give the narration less of a sense of intimacy.
- Past tense may give the narration less of a sense of immediacy.
- Summarization of the thinking may reduce both intimacy and immediacy.

DIRECT INTROSPECTION VS. INDIRECT INTROSPECTION

When you narrate a story in first person, all introspection will be in first person, whether direct or indirect. A shift in grammatical tense may occur (from present to past tense), but grammatical person doesn't change (first person in both cases), so you run little risk of distracting the reader.

In a story narrated in third person, past tense, however, the choice between using direct or indirect introspection raises the issue of narrative shift. Most of the story is narrated in third person, past tense. Indirect introspection is also presented in third person, past tense, so you run no risk of distracting the reader. For example (indirect introspection in italics),

> "Good morning, Bessie," said Jack to the family cow. He patted her on the side, set a three-legged stool next to her, took a seat, and placed a bucket under her udders. Taking an udder in each hand, he began to squeeze each in turn. Alternating streams of warm milk shot into the bucket then

suddenly stopped. Jack tugged at each udder in disbelief. He grabbed the other two udders and tried them. After a couple of squeezes, the milk stopped.

Jack's insides churned, and his head throbbed. He hurled the stool out the door. *He realized that the cow had gone dry. The family's livelihood depended upon the sale of the cow's milk. He wondered what they would do now. His mother always seemed to know what to do in a crisis. He would ask her.*

Potential trouble arises when direct introspection is used in a story narrated in third person, past tense. Direct introspection is presented in first person, present tense, so a shift to direct introspection requires a shift in both person and tense.[11] Whether this is advisable or not depends on the situation and how you handle introspection.

When narrating in third person, past tense with substantial distance from the character, a shift to direct introspection (first person, present tense) represents a shift toward intimacy, which may be desirable. For example (direct introspection in italics),

One morning Jack was milking his cow when she ran dry. *Oh, no, he thought. Our livelihood depends on the sale of this cow's milk. What are we to do now? My mother always seems to know what to do in a crisis. I'll ask Mama.*

In intimate third person, switching from third person to first person creates a narrative shift that may jar the reader.[12] For example,

"Good morning, Bessie," said Jack to the family cow. He patted her on the side, set a three-legged stool next to her, took a seat, and placed a bucket under her udders. Taking an udder in each hand, he began to squeeze each in turn. Alternating streams of warm milk shot into the bucket, then suddenly stopped. Jack tugged at each udder in disbelief. He grabbed the other two udders and tried them. After a couple of squeezes the milk stopped.

Jack's insides churned, and his head throbbed. He hurled the stool out the door. *Oh no, he thought, the cow has run dry. Our livelihood depends on the sale of this cow's milk. What are we to do now? My mother always seems to know what to do in a crisis. I'll ask Mama.*

The use of direct introspection in a story otherwise narrated in third person, past tense involves a shift in tense and grammatical person (to present tense and first person), which risks jarring the reader out of the story. Whether or not direct narration should be used in a story otherwise narrated in third person, past tense depends upon the situation, your objectives, and how you use attribution tags and thinking verbs.

EPIPHANY

An *epiphany* is a character's sudden realization or burst of insight. They are the "aha!" moments of introspection that put information in a new light. Epiphanies may be used to facilitate a turning point in the plot or to change the character.

Although epiphanies are technically introspection, they are often preceded by information not previously understood by the character. That new information may come from various sources, including dialogue or recollection. In an epiphany the character revises that information and sees it in a new light.

Here's an example (epiphany in italics).

> Fort pried another chunk of limestone from the mud and pitched it in the same direction as the first stone. He imagined the second stone falling right next to the first one. No way, he thought. Then he recalled his football coach teaching the team new plays, "What you can imagine—you can do." Fort cast another rock into the distance and visualized it falling next to the other two.
>
> He stopped. *Maybe he could use the same technique to control his temper.*

The moment this character puts it all together for a potential solution to his problem is an epiphany.

TAKEAWAYS

1. Introspection is a window into the character's mind and heart, providing you with a powerful tool for characterization.
2. A character's thoughts show his reasons for action, his motivation, thus improving the effectiveness of plot.
3. What a character thinks about the world around him adds depth to the story.
4. A character's introspection can help the reader see the world through different eyes, enhancing the story's theme.
5. Use plain type for introspection.
6. Attributions may be used to make clear who is doing the thinking.
7. Introspection may be embedded within a paragraph or constitute an entire paragraph.

8. Verbs of thought may be used to help identify who is thinking.
9. Introspection is usually presented in either past tense or present tense.
10. A character's thoughts are usually written in either first person or third person.
11. Introspection may be presented intimately or with distance.
12. *Direct introspection* uses the character's exact words.
13. *Indirect introspection* summarizes or paraphrases the thinker's words.
14. When most of a story is presented in third person, past tense, direct narration represents a narrative shift to first person, present tense, that risks jarring the reader.
15. An *epiphany* is a character's sudden realization or burst of insight that may be used to turn the plot or to change a character.

In this chapter we explored how a character thinks. The next chapter shows how to help a character recall important information.

4

RECOLLECTION

The fiction-writing mode that reveals what a character remembers.

CHAPTER CONTENTS
Timeline
Prompting recollection
Verbs of recollection
Recollection in scenes
Recollection in sequels
Recollection vs. flashbacks
Fragmentation
Choosing recollection

*R*ecollection is the fiction-writing mode whereby a character remembers something. A character may recall anything to which he has been previously exposed.

Wouldn't you love to have a perfect memory? As an author, you can portray your character recalling whatever she needs to remember, whenever she needs it. That may be from earlier in the story, as with a detective recalling a clue from the crime scene. A character may also recall an event from before the beginning of the story, such as a traumatic childhood experience, part of his backstory.

TIMELINE

To appreciate fully the role of recollection, you need to understand the time structure of a story. Aristotle is credited with being the first to recognize that stories have a structure based on their time-line: beginning, middle, and ending.[1] Today, that timeline should be updated as follows:

- Backstory
- Present story (including beginning, middle, ending)
- Future story (an implied future for the characters).

Backstory consists of events that precede the beginning of Chapter 1 and may be delivered via three different methods: (1) direct narration (from the all-seeing, all-knowing narrator), (2) expository devices (through props, such as a diary, a message in a bottle, or a treasure map), or (3) characters (via dialogue, introspection, or recollection).

Effective presentation of recollection involves many factors: triggering, verbs, recollection, flashbacks, fragmentation, and choices.

PROMPTING RECOLLECTION

Everyone has forgotten information squirreled away in the nooks and crannies of their mind. You need some sort of stimulus to bring that information to the conscious mind. Recollections may be triggered in two ways: self-prompting and from an outside stimulus.

A character might prompt recollection herself simply by thinking about a problem, just as in real life we ponder an issue and then recall information that has been stored in our subconscious. Sometimes that recollection is delayed by seconds, hours, or even days as the mind searches its memory banks.

Self-prompting may work fine for story situations where the character can think about an issue and wait while an answer presents itself. In such situations recollection may pull backstory into "the present" of a story by having a character recall information or events.

In other situations, having the solution-generating information pop into the character's mind may seem implausible. This may be especially problematic for key story decisions, such as if the information is recalled "in the nick of time" at the climax of the story. If recollection isn't appropriately triggered, the reader might justifiably ask why the character didn't think of it earlier.[2]

One solution is for an outside stimulus to trigger the recollection. That stimulation may come in a variety of forms, such as a statement from another character or a sensory experience (a sight, sound, taste, smell, or touch). Recollection may be triggered by anything that stimulates the character's mind to recall the information.

Examples of prompted recollection in fiction abound. In my young-adult novel *Cracks*, the main character is frustrated in his attempt to climb a rock wall that is too steep and smooth. He studies the wall and recalls tilted rock layers along roads cut through hills. This newly recalled information helps him devise a plan for success.

VERBS OF RECOLLECTION

As with other fiction-writing modes, specific verbs are associated with recollection. *Remembered, recalled, called to mind, thought back to, and reminisced* are verbs and phrases that indicate recollection. Here's an example using a verb of recollection (verb of recollection in italics).

> Jason paused before stepping into the diner. He *recalled* hearing how Bellows had killed a rival in Modesto. With an ice pick.

RECOLLECTION IN SCENES

Remember, a *scene* is a passage of writing in which a character attempts to achieve an objective. Depending on the nature of the story, a character may recall something at any point in a scene. It may be information that helps her achieve her objectives, or it may complicate or thwart her efforts. Because scenes are about action and should be relatively fast-paced, recollection tends to be brief, even fleeting. If such recollection is short and relevant to the scene, the reader may not notice a break in the action.

RECOLLECTION IN SEQUELS

While a scene shows a character attempting to achieve a goal, a *sequel* is what follows, a passage of writing in which the character reflects on the outcome of that preceding scene. Because the character is usually unsuccessful in a scene, a sequel often begins with her experiencing frustration. Recollection may be an important part of the thinking phase of sequels, when the character attempts to make sense of his predicament. Here's an example (recollection in italics).

Then Bodie remembered where he was. He scooted an elbow across the rock under him and rolled onto his side. His forehead throbbed, and he felt dizzy. He lay back again and carefully eased his head onto the rock floor. He blinked and forced himself to think and remember. *The opening of the cave had collapsed.* Now he was in total darkness, trapped. At least Spider couldn't get to him. Then he realized that Spider had probably already left him for dead.

Without Spider and Tug to worry about, he could just dig himself out, one rock at a time. It might take hours or days, but eventually he would get out. *Then he remembered the solid rock he had encountered during his frenzied digging.* Had that been the only way out? Or had he been confused? He listened for a clue about which way was out. Nothing.

Sequels present a potentially huge role for recollection. In sequels, recollection may be as long as necessary to review the relevant events that resulted in the character's current predicament.

RECOLLECTION VS. FLASHBACKS

Recollection is not a flashback, although they may have some things in common. Both recollections and flashbacks occur within the mind of the character; both may expose backstory; and both need to be triggered. The similarity between recollection and flashbacks ends there.

A flashback stops the forward progress of the story while the reader is taken back in time to experience a scene. For flashbacks to be effective, they must:

- Be significant enough to justify taking the reader on a detour from the main storyline.
- Use a transition to guide the reader into the backstory.
- Begin with a change of verb tense from simple past tense (He stopped by his friend's house) to past perfect (He had stopped by his friend's house).
- After transitioning the reader back in time, the character relives (in simple past tense) the scene in a dreamlike state.
- A flashback should be structured as a scene to have adequate impact, and that means it must be of sufficient length to do its job.
- The reader then transitions back to the present, with a brief return to past-perfect tense and a reminder that alerts the reader that the character's mind is back in the real-time of the story.

Recollection differs from a flashback in many ways. Recollection does not involve a change in time from the story's present to the backstory. Recollection does not relive the past. Recollection is not in a dreamlike experience; it's closer to the surface of the character's mind. Although it can sometimes be lengthy, recollection may also be concise. Recollection may be accomplished through verbs and verb phrases. Recollection requires no transition, while flashbacks require transitions both in and out of the backstory scene. Verbs of recollection require no change of tense (from simple past tense to past-perfect tense) to effect a transition.

FRAGMENTATION

Sometimes you may have the character recall only part of a situation or event. In *The Bourne Identity* by Robert Ludlum, Jason Bourne is an amnesia victim who recalls only fragments of his life as an assassin. In some cases, flashes of recollection portray partial memories.

CHOOSING RECOLLECTION

The craft of fiction is largely about making choices, and the decisions of how and when to use recollection are no exception. Here are situations when recollection may be the most appropriate tool:

- You wish to avoid direct narration
- Expository devices aren't practical
- A flashback scene isn't warranted
- Disruption of the story's momentum needs to be minimized

TAKEAWAYS

1. The timeline structure of a story includes backstory, present story (including beginning, middle, and ending), and future story.
2. In a novel, backstory consists of events that precede Chapter 1 and may be delivered through direct narration, expository devices, and characters.
3. Recollection may be triggered by self-prompting or by an outside stimulus.
4. Verbs and verb phrases of recollection include *remember, recall, call to mind, think back to,* and *reminisce.*
5. Recollection in scenes should be brief.
6. Recollection in sequels may be extensive.
7. Recollection and flashbacks have similarities and differences.
8. Fragmented recollection may generate partial memory.

9. Recollection may be the right tool when you wish to avoid direct narration; expository devices aren't practical; a flashback isn't warranted; and disruption of the story needs to be minimized.

We've spent the last four chapters within the mind of the character (sensation, emotion, introspection, and recollection). The next two chapters show how to portray events through action and summarization.

PART II

ACTIVITY

Two fiction-writing modes may be classified as *activity*, since they portray story events: action and summarization.

5

ACTION

The fiction-writing mode that shows things happening, in detail,
as they occur.

CHAPTER CONTENTS
Immediacy
Tense
Verbs: strong vs. weak
Active or passive voice
Action verbs and adverbs
Details
Chronological order
Stimulus-response order
Response-stimulus order
Incidental action
Quantity of action
Scenes vs. sequels

W hat's a surefire way to get your story moving? Put your
character into action. *Action* is the fiction-writing mode

used to show events, in detail, as they occur[1] to propel stories forward and make them exciting and realistic.

The mechanics of writing action depend upon the following issues: immediacy, tense, strong vs. weak verbs, active or passive voice, verbs and adverbs, details, chronological order, stimulus-response order, incidental action, and quantity of action.

IMMEDIACY

Immediacy is the degree to which a story seems to be unfolding now, giving the reader the illusion that he's experiencing the events of the story rather than hearing about them secondhand.[2] Immediacy ranges from delayed to immediate.

TENSE

In the action mode, the more an event is described as it is occuring, the more the reader feels he is living the story. Whenever a delay separates an event from its telling, the gap in time reduces immediacy. Grammatical tense largely determines the immediacy of portrayed events.

Stories have been told in *simple past tense* for centuries. As children we listened to stories being read aloud in simple past tense. Whatever the reason, *simple past tense* is very natural for storytelling. For example (past tense in italics),

George *purchased* meat from a local butcher, then *ran* home.

The vast majority of fiction is told in simple past tense. In effect, simple past tense is "story tense," or "fiction tense."

Present tense would seem to be the most natural tense to create immediacy. For example,

> George *purchases* meat from a local butcher and then *runs* home.

Present tense by definition possesses immediacy. But since most books are written in past tense, readers have come to expect it, so fiction in present tense seems awkward and unnatural.

Fiction may be told in any tense the author chooses, but most tenses create mismatches that reduce immediacy. *Future tense* lacks immediacy because the events have yet to occur. For example,

> George *will purchase* meat from a local butcher and then *will run* home.

Past-perfect tense creates an obvious delay in storytelling. For example,

> George *had purchased* meat from a local butcher and then *had run* home.

The helping verb in *past-perfect tense* reminds the reader that the event occurred in the past but not the *immediate* past. Although *past-perfect tense* has its uses (such as when events are summarized), its time-delayed nature renders it inappropriate for creating immediacy.

Simple past tense is the default tense for fiction.

VERBS: STRONG VS. WEAK

Which of the following sentences do you like best?

O'Roarke held the rope.
O'Roarke tightened his grip on the rope.

He put the plastic cap back onto the container and closed it.
He slipped the plastic cap back onto the container and
snapped it tight.

The horses moved out of the starting gate.
The horse charged out of the starting gate.

The first sentence in each pair above uses a weak verb: *held, put, closed,* and *moved.* The second sentence in each pair uses a strong verb: *tightened, slipped, snapped,* and *charged.*

Weak verbs communicate little of interest. Strong verbs are dynamic. The weakest of all are conjugations of the verb *to be (am, are, was, were, been),* because *to be* is a static state. Nothing happens —the subject just "is." Numerous other verbs are little better, offering lifeless generalities, such as *move, tend, lapse, seem.* Here's an example of description using a weak verb (*engage*).

Silas *engaged* his adversary in mortal combat.

Here's description using strong verbs (*parried* and *thrust*):

Silas *parried* the sword stroke with his musket, then *thrust*
his bayonet into the redcoat's chest.

Adverbs modify verbs by showing *how* action is performed. To improve description, you may be tempted to add an adverb to a weak verb. A better approach is to find a stronger verb. Instead of *She hit him hard,* write *She slugged him.*

ACTIVE OR PASSIVE VOICE

One of the first bits of advice offered to beginning writers is to use active voice rather than passive voice. In *active voice* the subject of the sentence performs the action of the verb: the subject is active. For example,

Hansel ran.

The child cried.

Mike laughed.

The verbs in each example above are *intransitive verbs* (they express action but do not have objects). The issue of passive voice comes into play with the use of *transitive verbs* (the verb expresses action and is followed by an object, either a noun or a pronoun).[3] Here's an example of a transitive verb in active voice.

Hansel shoved the witch.

The same sentence may be expressed in passive voice.

The witch was shoved by Hansel.

Active voice describes action as it is happening in the real time of the story. Passive voice is not as strong or immediate because the object is acted upon *indirectly*, slightly delaying the action described. For example, *Moby Dick capsized the boat* is immediate action. But, *The boat was capsized by Moby Dick* is delayed, indirect reporting of the action. Passive voice slows the pace and adds words to the sentence (compare *capsized* to *was capsized by*).

To convert a sentence from passive voice to active voice, identify who or what is performing the action and move it to the beginning of the sentence.

> Grandma was eaten by the wolf. (Passive voice)
> The wolf ate Grandma. (Active voice)

Passive voice isn't grammatically incorrect and may be appropriate for a variety of reasons, such as to slow the pace, to redirect emphasis, to create a sense of mystery, or to infuse a tone of detachment.

Compared to words at the beginning or in the middle, the last words in a sentence tend to receive the most notice. Passive voice presents an opportunity to redirect emphasis. The sentence *Detective Hiller told the guests that Mr. Slade was shot by the butler* emphasizes the butler, while *Detective Hiller told the guests that the butler shot Mr. Slade* emphasizes Mr. Slade.

Passive voice may also be helpful in creating a sense of mystery, as in *Mr. Slade was shot.* Here, the name of the shooter is omitted, possibly because at this point in the story, the perpetrator is unknown, or the writer doesn't want to reveal this information.

Passive voice may also be used when it is not important who performed the action or to create a tone of detachment, as in *The rats were euthanized.*

ACTION VERBS AND ADVERBS

In action mode the goal is to create clear mental images of events. That means using the most appropriate verb, preferably without the aid of a modifier to show how action is performed; i.e., an *adverb*. Consider the following.

Silas *was walking painfully* toward the river.

A weak verb provides the reader with only a murky mental image. Eliminating *to be* derivatives in a sentence strengthens the action and thus its immediacy. For example,

Silas *walked painfully* toward the river.

In the example above, eliminating *was* strengthened the sentence, but *walked* is such a generic verb it must be supported by the adverb *painfully* to create the desired image. A more specific verb adds clarity. For example,

Silas *limped* painfully toward the river.

Limped creates a more vivid image but the adverb *painfully* dilutes the verb by its very presence, drawing attention to the apparent need to strengthen the verb. Recasting the sentence without the adverb creates more immediate action.

Silas *limped* toward the river, each step sending jolts of pain through his leg.

Create immediate action by using strong, specific, image-creating verbs, while avoiding adverbs.

DETAILS

In real life, an "adrenaline moment" heightens our awareness and prepares us to fight or flee. In the action fiction-writing mode, the character experiences an elevated sense of awareness that illuminates details of the events and surroundings. That sense of awareness needs relevant details to bring the passage to life.

Specific, relevant details help the reader to be there—to experience the moment, the drama. Not just any details will do. In the heat of a battle, details of weapons clashing would be appropriate, but details describing the wildflowers crushed underfoot would probably not be relevant.

Too many details can stall a story and distract the reader. We're looking for details that matter, sometimes referred to as *telling* details. Compare the following examples.

> Through the fog Lemuel saw a redcoat thrust a bayonet-tipped musket toward him. Lemuel deflected the attack and hit the redcoat.

The example above is an action-packed passage, but it lacks details that could bring it to life. Consider the following example.

> Out of the fog a redcoat thrust his bayonet-tipped musket toward Lemuel's chest. Lemuel swung his rifle at the musket. The two weapons clashed. Using all his strength, Lemuel swung the butt of his rifle into the redcoat's jaw.

Here, additional details brought life to the action:

- The bayonet was aimed at Lemuel's chest.
- He swung his rifle to block the attack.

- Weapons clashed.
- Lemuel used all his strength.
- He swung the butt of his rifle into the coat's jaw.

The relevance of detail matters. Consider the following.

> Out of the fog a half-dressed redcoat thrust his bayonet-tipped "Brown Bess" musket toward Lemuel's chest. Lemuel stepped over a rabbit hiding in the grass and swung the Kentucky rifle he'd inherited from his father at the musket. The two weapons clashed like thunderclaps. After carefully considering his alternatives, Lemuel swung the butt of his rifle into the redcoat's jaw.

In the above example, the following details are irrelevant (and distracting) in the context of this action:

- The redcoat was half-dressed.
- The musket was a "Brown Bess."
- A rabbit was in the grass.
- Lemuel's weapon was a Kentucky rifle.
- The rifle was inherited from his father.
- The weapons clashed like thunderclaps.
- Lemuel carefully considered his alternatives.

To bring action to life, add only vivid, relevant details.

CHRONOLOGICAL ORDER

In the action mode, events are usually presented in chronological order, so that one item follows another exactly as they occur in time.[4] For example,

> Queequeg grabbed the harpoon, drew it back, then hurled it into the side of the whale.

Writing in chronological order might seem obvious, but presenting events as if they are *simultaneous* is an easy trap to fall into.

> Grabbing the harpoon, Queequeg drew it back and hurled it into the side of the whale.

In the example above, the separate acts of grabbing, drawing back, and hurling are presented as if they all occurred at the same time. As is the case in the example above, simultaneity[5] may be an unintended consequence of recasting sentences to avoid repetition of sentence construction. Avoiding repetition is an admirable goal, but it may lead to awkward, confusing, or unintended simultaneous action.

Although there are occasions when actions can and should be shown simultaneously, be cautious when starting sentences with words ending with *-ing*. Phrases structured in this manner (present participle phrases) signal to the reader that the action in the introductory phrase happens *at the same time as* action in the main body of the sentence. For example,

> Holding his breath, Silas aimed the musket.

Here, Silas is simultaneously holding his breath and aiming. These two actions *can* be done at the same time.

The same caution applies to sentences starting with phrases that begin with time-sensitive prepositions (such as *as, while, at the same time*):

As Silas held his breath, he aimed the musket.

Again, no problem, because holding your breath may be accomplished at the same time as aiming a musket. But beginning sentences with time-sensitive prepositions or words ending with -*ing* may produce undesirable results. Consider the following:

Loading his musket, Silas aimed and squeezed the trigger.

At first glance this sentence might seem acceptable. But loading a musket and firing it are two separate actions, so Silas cannot load his musket and aim it at the same time. We want to show each action in proper sequence to provide a clear image of the event. For example,

Silas loaded his musket, aimed, then squeezed the trigger.

Structuring actions as simultaneous may result in physical impossibilities.[6] For example,

Racing across the street, Marshall McCabe untied the outlaw, shoved him into the jail cell, locked the door, and poured himself a cup of coffee.

Whew! Only a character with superhuman powers could do all that simultaneously.

Simultaneous action is okay if it's realistically possible, and it's acceptable for incidental action that warrants only a dependent clause. *Incidental action* includes small amounts of activity, such as in gestures, mannerisms, and body language. (A dependent clause is a group of words that contains a subject and verb but does not express a complete thought. A dependent clause cannot stand alone as a sentence.) For example,

> As he scratched his head, Newton contemplated the fallen apple.

In the above example, *As he scratched his head* is incidental action, and it's presented in a dependent clause.

Placing action in a dependent clause diminishes its importance. For example,

> As the long line of redcoats charged, Lieutenant Smith screamed, "Fire!"

In the action mode something as dramatic as a bayonet charge warrants chronological treatment and an independent clause, so it doesn't seem incidental or offhand. For example,

> The long line of redcoats charged.
> Lieutenant Smith screamed, "Fire!"

In the action mode, events are usually presented in chronological order. Begin sentences with a time-sensitive preposition or a word ending with *-ing* only when you intend for actions to be simultaneous. Remember that placing action within a dependent clause diminishes its importance.

STIMULUS-RESPONSE ORDER

The action mode is about things happening, but not just any old things in any old ways. Action must make sense. Someone does something for a reason, and then someone responds: (1) action meets resistance, and then there is a reaction; or (2) action meets acceptance, and then there is a reaction.

The logic of action-mode writing is cause and effect, also called stimulus and response[7].

In most action writing, stimulus precedes response. For example,

Silas sipped, and he swallowed.

Rachel asked. George answered.

A bullet hit Hadjo, and he fell.

Although most action writing works best if the response follows the corresponding stimulus, there is an important exception. In *The Marshall Plan for Getting Your Novel Published*, Evan Marshall states, "To show a character's reaction to something shocking, show the reaction before describing what is being reacted to." In these situations, "You'll create a more dramatic effect if you have your character react first, then describe what it is he has seen."[8]

As explained by Marshall, "This technique works for a couple of reasons. First, a tiny moment of suspense is created between the horrified reaction and the description of what's being seen. Second, a truly awful spectacle will most likely require a good amount of description. If you describe the spectacle at length, then show your character's reaction, there's the danger of creating an odd, delayed-reaction effect that is not desirable."[9]

Consider the following:

The earth and air thumped with the boom of cannon. Silas flinched.

This is in classic stimulus-response order, but having the character react after such dramatic stimulus is anticlimactic. The problem gets even worse as the description gets longer. For example,

> The earth and air thumped with the boom of cannon, and smoke billowed from one of the British field pieces. Silas flinched.

Now let's reverse the order.

> Silas flinched. The earth and air thumped with the boom of cannon. Smoke billowed from one of the British field pieces.

Here, the character reacts by flinching before he is consciously aware of the stimulus. In real life there are times when we respond before we are aware of the stimulus. In school, did you ever jump when someone slammed a desktop? Have you ever jerked half out of your seat in a movie theater? The body responds reflexively to dramatic stimulus before the conscious mind interprets the cause.

With the exception of a character reacting instinctively to something shocking, show action in stimulus-response order.

INCIDENTAL ACTION

Action can be presented in large portions as in a *scene,* where a character attempts to achieve a goal. Action may also be shown in small amounts, such as in gestures, mannerisms, and body language.

These incidental bits of activity have various uses. They may help define characters, control rhythm and pace, show a character's emotion, demonstrate a physical reaction to a stimulus, or connect the character to the setting. Consider the following example:

> Travis held the rope snug against his backside.

Taken as is, this passage may accomplish your objective. But adding a little incidental action can produce a more vivid image.

> Travis held the rope snugly against his backside and braced himself.

and braced himself is incidental action, but it adds meaning and impact to the sentence. Something is *going to* happen. Relocating the action can change the sentence's rhythm:

> Travis *braced himself* and held the rope snugly against his backside.

Relocating the action may change the emphasis of the sentence.

> *Bracing himself,* Travis held the rope snugly against his backside.

Action may be used to connect the character to the setting.

> Bracing himself *against a tree,* Travis held the rope snugly against his backside.

Or a bit of action may be used to change the meaning of the sentence entirely.

> Travis held the rope *and chuckled.*

QUANTITY OF ACTION

If action is what brings fiction to life, why not write everything in the action mode? Because unremitting action can tire the reader. If you're like me, you've been to movies with hardly a break between action sequences. Long before the film is over, I'm exhausted and ready to head for the exit.

No one could question the importance of action in fiction, but too much action at one time deadens the reader to it, thus reducing its impact. You need to carefully orchestrate action to provide breathers or natural pauses.

Action is organized as *scenes* and the breathers as *sequels*. Action dominates scenes, while sequels tend to be reflective. (A *sequel* is what follows a scene—an aftermath, a regrouping, a breather, a recovery). Scenes are not one-hundred percent action. Action is not the right tool for every job. Remember, there are ten other fiction-writing modes, and each has its role.

TAKEAWAYS

1. *Immediacy* is the degree to which a story unfolds as it is being told.
2. Simple past tense is the "story tense," the default tense for fiction.
3. Use strong verbs instead of weak verbs.
4. In *active voice* the subject performs the action of the verb.
5. Create immediate action by using strong, specific, image-creating verbs, while generally avoiding adverbs.
6. Specific, relevant details help the reader to experience the moment.
7. In action mode, events are usually told in chronological order.

8. In most action writing, stimulus precedes response.
9. When showing something shocking, it's often best to show the response before stimulus.
10. *Incidental action* includes gestures, mannerisms, and body language.
11. Action is organized into scenes.
12. Sequels provide an aftermath.

In the next chapter we'll address an incredibly useful fiction-writing mode that compresses action: summarization.

6

SUMMARIZATION

The fiction-writing mode that restates actions or events.

CHAPTER CONTENTS
"Show. Don't tell."
Reporting events
Shifting time or location
Setting up a new passage or viewpoint
Varying rhythm and pace

Action mode *shows* an event in detail as it happens—summarization *tells* about it. The old writing axiom "Show, don't tell." implies that summarization is inferior writing, to be discouraged. This is unfortunate because telling in the form of summarization has a vital role. *Summarization* is the fiction-writing mode whereby story events are recapped. In summarization mode, events are told rather than shown.

Any event may be portrayed either in the action mode or in summarization. Consider the following gunfight in action mode.

As the sun reached its zenith, Cisco strode onto the dusty street and faced Bart. Without warning, Bart reached for his pistol. Cisco dived to the right as Bart fired. Cisco rolled in the dirt and drew his Peacemaker. He fanned his hand across the Colt's hammer in rapid succession, sending three slugs into Bart's chest.

The same event may be summarized as:

At noon, Cisco faced Bart and gunned him down in the street.

Summary mode has many applications. It may be used to: (1) report an event that doesn't warrant the detailed, as-it-happens treatment of the action mode; (2) shift from one time or location to another; (3) introduce a passage by "catching up" the reader on what has happened since the previous scene, sequel, chapter, or section; or (4) vary rhythm and pace.[1]

REPORTING EVENTS

Summary mode is appropriate for reporting events that don't warrant detailed, real-time presentation. As fiction writers we make many decisions. We choose which events to report and which to leave out. We decide which events to report in detail and which to summarize. For example, depending on our objectives, a *summary* of the gunfight between Cisco and Bart may be appropriate. Readers may need to know that the event occurred but not the details. They may need to be reminded of an event. *Telling* lets readers speed past less important action. If fiction were a video player, action would be accessed with the Play button, and summarization would be the Fast-forward button.

Summarization may be particularly appropriate when there is repetition of events.[2] For example, if the confrontation with Bart was one of five gunfights Cisco had that day, showing each of those events in action mode could become tedious for the reader.

SHIFTING TIME OR LOCATION

Summarization provides an opportunity to telescope time and shift location. Rather than showing all the details in an uninteresting journey, the writer might summarize it. For example,

> As the storm continued over the next three hours, they followed the winding path around and over one dark hill after another.

Summarization can transport a character across time and space.

SETTING UP A NEW PASSAGE OR VIEWPOINT CHARACTER

A *setup* sets the stage, informing the reader of the circumstances under which the following passage begins. You may use summarization to introduce a new scene, sequel, chapter, or section. In novels with multiple characters from whose viewpoint the story is told, summarization might help establish a new viewpoint character. This may be accomplished at the beginning of the new passage by naming the new viewpoint character and describing what he is doing, thinking, or feeling. For example:

> Pike reached the top of the hill and stopped. Before him, as far as he could see, stretched rolling, grass-covered hills.

VARYING RHYTHM AND PACE

As you saw with the gunfight between Cisco and Bart, summarization and action, even when used to describe the same event, have a different pace and rhythm. The decision to use one versus the other becomes a tool for manipulating the story. For example, imagine a medieval battle with knights engaged in a series of swordfights. You might decide to describe the first fight in action mode, summarize the next three, during which Arthur dispatches three more dark knights, and then show the climactic fight in gory detail.

As with each of the other ten fiction-writing modes, summarization has both advantages and disadvantages. Action involves the reader and is intimate and immediate. Summarization distances readers and lacks immediacy, but it spares them from reading details of redundant, unimportant, or tedious events. Summarization offers one distinct advantage over the action mode —brevity.

The action and summarization modes are two means of presenting story events. Summarization deserves respect as a fiction-writing mode. For any particular passage of fiction, you must decide when to show and when to tell.

TAKEAWAYS

1. Any event may be portrayed in either action mode or in summarization.
2. Summary mode is appropriate for reporting events that don't warrant detailed, real-time presentation.
3. Summarization provides an opportunity to telescope time and shift location.

4. A *setup* informs the reader of the circumstances under which the following passage begins.
5. As compared to the action mode, summarization provides an opportunity to change pace and rhythm.

Let's move on to the next chapter, which covers a character's speech, or conversation.

PART III

DIALOGUE

One fiction-writing mode represents a character's speech, whether it is dialogue or monologue: conversation.

7

CONVERSATION

The fiction-writing mode that presents characters talking.

CHAPTER CONTENTS
What the character speaks about
What the character's speech reveals about this thinking
How the character speaks

W hat's the difference between the fiction-writing mode *conversation* and the term *dialogue*? Nothing. Each of the ten other fiction-writing modes ends with the suffix *-tion*, so for the sake of consistency when compiling the modes, I felt obligated to find a comparable name for dialogue.

The fiction-writing mode of *conversation* represents characters talking: dialogue and monologue. What a character says and how he says it can reveal a huge amount about that character's personality and who he really is. Dialogue also adds immediacy to fiction, and can provide rhythm, change pace, create tone, present information, or summarize events.

A character's own words bring her to life by defining her background, personality, values, attitude, motivation, and goals. The keys to developing character through dialogue include: (1) *what* the character talks about, (2) what the character's speech reveals about her *thinking*, and (3) *how* the character speaks.

WHAT THE CHARACTER SPEAKS ABOUT

Why does the subject matter of dialogue contribute to characterization? Most of what the character talks about is a reflection of the story's plot. In a mystery, for example, the character would talk most about solving the crime. But what a character speaks about also reveals his nature, who he is inside.[1] Here's an example.

> "So you're a dealer?" asked Aaron. "How can you do that?"
> He stabbed the knife deep into the log and let it stand.
> Trent shrugged. "Guys like Rudy want the stuff. I provide it. It's supply and demand."
> "Pusher," said Aaron, almost spitting out the word.

Here, as Aaron expresses his disapproval of Trent's lifestyle, he simultaneously reveals his own character. Aaron isn't just talking about illegal drugs—he's also exposing his character.

WHAT THE CHARACTER'S SPEECH REVEALS ABOUT HIS THINKING

How do you learn about a character's thinking when he speaks? A character's speech largely reflects his thoughts. If the character intentionally thinks one thing but says another, that also reveals something about his nature. Dialogue provides a window to the character's mind, and *how* the character thinks reveals much about who that character is.[2] Is he intelligent, poorly educated, or ignorant? Rational or insane? Logical or twisted? Open-minded or prejudiced? Speech reflects a character's thought process.

> "I'm an entrepreneur, a businessman. I fill a public need and make a buck for myself. Hey guys," said Trent with a chuckle, "it's the American way."
> Aaron scowled. "You make me sick."

Here, Trent's words reveal his view of life, how he rationalizes his behavior. Aaron's speech reveals his intolerance of Trent's behavior.

HOW THE CHARACTER SPEAKS

Have you ever read fiction where all the characters sound alike? As authors we each tend to write in much the same style as we personally think and speak. Unless you make an effort to create distinct voices for each character, their speech will sound very similar. And more than likely, they will all sound like you.

Creating characters who all sound the same shows a lack of effort on your part to differentiate them. They may all sound alike because they *are* alike. Unique individuals in a story, each with his own voice, add depth to it.

Characters in a story may range from major to minor to incidental. The larger the role, the more that character's personality should be developed. But even if an incidental character has only a single line of dialogue, that one line may be enough to differentiate her from others and bring her to life.

Ideally, if character names were hidden, the reader could still tell who is speaking.[3] Characters need to be distinct, but not just for the sake of being eccentric. Each character's unique qualities should reflect his role in the story.[4] Is he from the East Coast or the Midwest? Is he uptight or lackadaisical? Is he a fast thinker or dimwitted? Many factors contribute to a character's speech pattern:

- Words (word choice, contractions, unnecessary words)
- Sentences (structure, diction, phrasing, fragments, grammar, dropping of words, word order)
- Rhythm and pace (cadence)
- Voice quality (inflection, pitch, timbre, enunciation, volume)
- Accent (pronunciations, dialect, colloquialisms)
- Trendiness (contemporary or archaic slang or figures of speech)
- Profanity (vulgar, insulting, disparaging, or racist language)
- Coherence (straightforward, disjointed, misdirected, or speaking at cross-purposes)

As complicated as this might sound, a single line may go far in distinguishing a character's speech. Consider the following:

"How despicably I have behaved."

"I screwed up."

"Not one of my finer moments, to be sure."

"My bad!"

Which of the above statements would you match to (1) a teenager, (2) a golfer, (3) a longshoreman, or (4) an English lady?

TAKEAWAYS

1. What a character speaks about reveals her nature.
2. A character's speech reflects her thoughts and her thought processes.
3. Unless you make an effort to create a distinct voice for each of your characters, their speech will sound very similar.

Fortunately for fiction *readers* there is much to learn from the conversation of characters. Fortunately for fiction *writers*, we have plenty of tools for developing characters through dialogue.

In addition to characterization, effective presentation of conversation, or dialogue, includes

- Effectively advancing the plot
- Increasing or decreasing conflict
- Clearly identifying the speaker
- The judicious use of verbs and adverbs of attribution
- Using attributions to control rhythm and pace
- Making speech sound natural
- Using correct punctuation

Each of these techniques will be explored in the following chapters.

8

ADVANCING PLOT THROUGH ACTION AND DIALOGUE

CHAPTER CONTENTS
Scenes
Scenes without action
Scenes without dialogue
Advantages of each
Facial expressions
Gestures
Movement
Violence

Nothing moves the story forward as well as a good scene. During the process of creating a scene, you may draw upon a variety of fiction-writing modes, including healthy doses of action and dialogue.

Technically, you don't need action to create a scene. Here's an example of a scene fragment from a fictional poker game.

"You must think I was born yesterday," said Bart. "I know a bluff when I see one. I call your bet."

Cisco said, "Read 'em and weep, pardner."

"Nobody's that lucky," said Bart.

"Careful now," said Cisco. "Them's fightin' words."

"Careful, my ass! You cheat."

"Reach for the sky," said Cisco, "or I'll put a slug in you."

"Now hold on," said Bart. "You wouldn't shoot a man in cold blood, would you?"

"Maybe we should step into the street," said Cisco, "and settle this like gentlemen."

It's also possible to create a scene solely with action and no dialogue, as in the following example.

Bart studied Cisco's face. With a sneer, Bart called the bet.

Cisco spread his cards on the table, revealing four aces.

Bart glared at Cisco, clenched his teeth, and reached inside his coat.

Cisco pulled his six-shooter.

Bart raised his hands.

With a wolfish grin, Cisco glared at Bart and nodded toward the door.

This example shows that without dialogue, a scene may lack depth and miss opportunities to engage and inform the reader. Let's try the same scene with both dialogue and action.

Bart studied Cisco's face. "You must think I was born yesterday. I know a bluff when I see one." With a sneer, he added, "I call your bet."

"Read 'em and weep, pardner," said Cisco as he spread his cards on the table, revealing four aces.

Bart glared at Cisco. "Nobody's that lucky."

"Careful now," said Cisco. "Them's fightin' words."

"Careful, my ass! You cheat." He clenched his teeth and reached inside his coat.

Cisco pulled his six-shooter. "Reach for the sky, or I'll put a slug in you."

Bart raised his hands. "Now hold on. You wouldn't shoot a man in cold blood, would you?"

Cisco glared with a wolfish grin and nodded toward the door. "Maybe we should step into the street and settle this like gentlemen."

Here, dialogue and action complement each other. Symbiotically, they create a richer, more satisfying experience for the reader, who can not only hear but visualize the events.

Within a scene that is heavy on action, the addition of dialogue may serve a variety of plot purposes: introducing a different train of thought, adding drama, changing emotions, dropping a pretense. For example,

"Maybe we should step into the street," said Cisco, "and settle this like gentlemen." Then with a smirk, he said, "Unless you're yellow."

Here, the example introduces a new consideration: cowardice. It also raises the stakes, because if Bart refuses to face Cisco in a gunfight, he will all but admit he is afraid.

Action within dialogue can range from subtle to substantial.

FACIAL EXPRESSIONS

- Raising an eyebrow
- Sneering
- Frowning
- Squinting

GESTURES

- Pointing a finger or steepling the hands
- Making a fist
- Pounding a table
- Holding hands up to surrender
- Crossing arms in front of chest
- Raising hands in resignation or despair

MOVEMENT

- Crossing a room
- Pushing back from a desk or table
- Edging closer

VIOLENCE

- Throwing a punch
- Firing a gun
- Blowing something up[1]

You may work action into dialogue in several ways. One is to include action in the same sentence as the dialogue. Where the action is placed within a sentence depends on the writer's objectives and style. For example,

> Pulling off his gauntlet, the knight said, "I will stand thy blow, if thou wilt stand mine."

Here, the emphasis is on "stand mine" since it is at the end of the sentence. Let's try another example.

> "I will stand thy blow, if thou wilt stand mine," said the knight, pulling off his gauntlet.

Since "pulling off his gauntlet" is at the end of the sentence, it commands greater emphasis.

Placing the action in midsentence changes the rhythm and emphasis by causing a pause or delay in the dialogue. For example,

> "I will stand thy blow," said the knight, pulling off his gauntlet, "if thou wilt stand mine."

TAKEAWAYS

1. Scenes advance the story.
2. Scenes may be written solely with dialogue.
3. Scenes may be written solely with action.
4. Using both dialogue and action offers advantages.
5. Action within dialogue may range from facial expressions and gestures to violence.
6. Action may be worked into dialogue at the beginning of the sentence, at the end, or in the middle.

In the next chapter we will explore ways to increase conflict with dialogue.

9

DIALOGUE TO INCREASE CONFLICT

CHAPTER CONTENTS
Formula for creating conflict
Parallel dialogue
On-the-nose dialogue
Oblique dialogue
Subtext dialogue
Silence

How can you use dialogue to create conflict? The basis of drama is conflict, and conflict begins with a character. For a character to be interesting, he must desire something, but unless the character acts to achieve his goal, he's just dreaming. Not just any goal will do—the goal must be important to the character. Achieving the goal, failing to achieve the goal, or even attempting to achieve the goal must have consequences, thus raising the stakes. Raising the stakes is important, but that's still not enough to create conflict. Only when the striving character encounters resistance to his effort does conflict arise.

The formula for creating conflict is Character + Goal + Stakes +Attempt + Resistance = Conflict. For example, Captain Ahab (character) wants to kill Moby Dick (goal). Ahab risks his ship, his life, and his crew (stakes) to get revenge. Great distances, the sea, the weather, Starbuck, and Moby Dick (resistance) all thwart Ahab's attempts, thus causing conflict throughout the story.

Often the character's effort to achieve his goal is physical (as in trying to catch bank robbers), but the effort may also be verbal (as in a town marshal's speech to recruit volunteers for a posse). For dialogue to create conflict, a character must have a goal. He verbalizes what he wants, hopeful that talking about it will help his endeavor. For example, he requests information, affection, assistance, favors, or tangible items. Wanting something and asking for it do not by themselves create conflict, however. The character must meet resistance; someone must say no or disagree.

The following scene provides an example of how dialogue can generate conflict.

> Marshal Webster raised his hand to silence the saloon-hall crowd. "Butch and his gang have robbed the bank. I'm forming a posse to track 'em down. Who'll ride with me?"
> "Not me, Marshal. The last posse to go after Butch got shot to pieces."
> "I shouldn't have to remind you," said Webster, "that the life savings of many of your neighbors was in that bank."
> "Fine," yelled a man. "Let them ride after Butch."
> "What about the widows and orphans?" asked Webster.
> "Sorry, Marshal, that's why the town hired you."

In this example, Marshal Webster wants to form a posse (goal) to catch the robbers and retrieve the bank deposits of widows and orphans (stakes). He pleads for help (attempt), but he is denied (resistance).

PARALLEL DIALOGUE

The example above demonstrates *parallel dialogue*, where each line of one character's statement responds to the previous line of the other character's statement.[1] One character asks a question or makes a statement, and the other character answers the question or follows up with a statement.

ON-THE-NOSE DIALOGUE

The example above also illustrates *on-the-nose*[2] or *direct*[3] dialogue, where characters say exactly what they mean,[4] with no attempt to demur, deceive, be witty, use subterfuge, etc.[5]

Parallel, on-the-nose dialogue that creates conflict may be viewed as an act of bartering or a tug of war[6] that boils down to a simple exchange: "I want something." And, "No, you can't have it." Or even simpler, "Please" and "No."[7] Conflict only arises if a character's attempt to achieve a goal meets resistance.

On-the-nose, parallel dialogue has an important role as characters try to outmaneuver each other on a verbal battlefield.[8] This type of dialogue can feature a variety of weapons including questions, anger, insults, and name-calling.[9] Such confrontations may be useful in illustrating the dynamics of a relationship as one character tries to seduce another, attempts to convince another of an unwelcome truth, or fends off accusations.[10]

OBLIQUE DIALOGUE

The opposite of parallel dialogue is *oblique dialogue,* sometimes called *misdirected dialogue,*[11] where characters (1) talk at cross-purposes,[12] (2) answer unasked questions,[13] (3) provide "answers" that really aren't,[14] (4) change subjects without warning,[15] or (5) carry on more than one conversation at a time.[16]

Taken out of context oblique dialogue might be confusing to a reader, so let's continue with the example of Marshal Webster's attempt to raise a posse.

> Webster paused and studied the crowd. "Who'll ride with me?"
> Someone asked, "Marshal, ain't you ever gonna marry the schoolmarm?"
> The men in the saloon snickered.
> "Yeah, and there's too many hogs roamin' the streets. What're you gonna do about that?"
> Hoots of laughter rolled through the crowd.

Oblique dialogue reflects real life in that we often don't listen to each other. Conversations can become little more than interrupted monologues,[17] where each person (1) focuses on what she wants; (2) is intent on her own message, rather than anyone else's; or (3) responds incompletely, if at all, to what is said to her.[18]

This type of dialogue may create conflict to the extent that oblique responses frustrate a character's attempt to achieve her goal.

SUBTEXT DIALOGUE

The opposite of on-the-nose dialogue (the character speaks his mind) is *subtext dialogue,*[19] where what characters say and what they really mean are different things.[20] Instead of what they mean, people (1) use language to manipulate each other, (2) withhold information and feelings, or (3) hint at things.[21]

Consider the following:

> Webster paused and studied the crowd. "Who'll ride
> with me?"
> "Marshal, have you ever led a posse that actually caught the
> robbers?"
> "What are you implying?" asked Webster.
> "Butch has a twenty-minute head start."

Here, the responses to Webster's request disguise the questioners' real concerns:

1. Based upon previous experience, are you competent to lead a posse?
2. We don't really want to chase the robbers, and we'll invent excuses not to join your posse; i.e., "It's already too late."

Subtext dialogue may create conflict to the extent the gap between what is said and what is not said[22] frustrates the character's attempt to achieve his goal.

SILENCE

Silence can also contribute to conflict by frustrating a character's attempt to achieve his goal. Silence can also add tension and suspense to dialogue by creating uncertainty and by postponing the outcome.[23] Also note that when a previously noisy environment quiets, even the most subtle sounds seem magnified. For example:

Marshal Webster studied the crowd. "Who'll ride with me?" The crowd fell silent. A chair squeaked at the back of the room. The clock behind the bar ticked the seconds away.

TAKEAWAYS

1. The formula for creating conflict is Character + Stakes + Goal + Attempt + Resistance = Conflict.
2. A character's attempt to achieve his goal may be physical, but the attempt and the resistance may also be oral.
3. In *parallel dialogue*, each line of one character's speech responds to the previous line of another character's words.
4. In *on-the-nose dialogue*, characters say exactly what they mean, with no attempt to demur, deceive, be witty, use subterfuge, etc.
5. In *oblique dialogue*, characters talk at cross-purposes, answer unasked questions, provide "answers" that really aren't, change subjects without warning, or carry on more than one conversation at a time.
6. In *subtext dialogue*, instead of what they mean, characters use language to manipulate each other, withhold information and feelings, or hint at things.
7. Silence can also contribute to conflict by frustrating the character's attempt to achieve his goal.

Dialogue can play a key role in creating conflict. Fortunately, writers have a well-stocked arsenal of techniques available to create that effect.

In the next chapter, we'll discuss how to indicate the speakers in dialogue.

A GIFT FROM WRITER TO WRITER

"Develop a passion for learning. If you do, you Will never cease to grow."

— ANTHONY J. D'ANGELO

I teach writing because I love watching new writers discover their potential. I meet many people who know they have some degree of talent, but few of them understand exactly how much potential they have until they amass all the tools they need to craft their best work. The eleven fiction-writing modes are big ones. Most writers know some of them, but rarely do I work with someone who's familiar with all of them, and that means that they're trying to work without a full toolkit. As Hemmingway said, we're all apprentices in the craft of writing, and I think this is one of the most exciting things about it. It's a never-ending journey of learning and perfecting our skills, but this is impossible without a full toolkit, and I love equipping new writers with these tools so that they can keep on pursuing the craft and discovering what they're really capable of. For me, this is as exciting as writing itself.

I've yet to find a book or a writing course that fully discusses all eleven fiction-writing modes, and I feel it's my duty to help as many writers as I can to explore them—hence the reason you're reading this book, and hence the reason I'd like to ask you a favor now that we're halfway through. You can help more writers to get to know these eleven modes and equip themselves with the tools they need to discover their full potential as fiction writers simply by leaving your review online.

By leaving a review of this book on Amazon, you'll attract the attention of other writers and help them to find this information—information that I believe is crucial to their success as fiction writers.

Every good writer understands that there's always more to know, and they're always looking to improve their skills and deepen their knowledge. Your review will help them to find a piece of the puzzle that many writers miss out on.

Thank you so much for your support. You're giving a gift that other writers will truly appreciate.

Scan the QR code below

10

IDENTIFYING THE SPEAKER

CHAPTER CONTENTS
Attributions
Character voice
Direct address
Context
Paragraphs

A s a reader, have you ever had to backtrack through dialogue to figure out who was speaking? We've all experienced this, and there's no excuse for it. Fiction writers have plenty of tools for indicating the speaker in dialogue: attributions, character voice, direct address, and context.

ATTRIBUTIONS

Attributions, also known as *dialogue tags*, are those words authors slip into dialogue to let the reader know who is speaking. For example,

"The sky is blue," he said.

Daniel said, "I love the way you cut your hair."

"Captain," Samuel said, "the wind has changed."

CHARACTER VOICE

Memorable characters each have a voice that reflects their uniqueness—their age, background, attitudes, etc. When a character has a voice distinctive from the other characters in the story, no further help may be needed to identify the speaker. Consider the following examples of how different jury members, each with a distinct voice, might say the same thing.

"The preponderance of both factual and circumstantial evidence suggests beyond a reasonable doubt that the accused did, in fact, perpetrate this heinous act of premeditated homicide."

"The evidence would seem to point, pretty clearly, to a guilty verdict."

"Face it, the son of a bitch killed her."

"Guilty! Guilty! Guilty!"

"Like, can we vote now to, like, hang the dude?"

DIRECT ADDRESS

One way to identify speakers in dialogue is to have the characters address each other by name, kinship, or title. For example,

"Andy, I'm heading back to town."

"Okay, Son, I'll catch up to you in the morning."

"Be careful, Sergeant. I smell trouble brewing."

While this technique may be effective in identifying the speaker, it can quickly become tiring, and it's not how real people usually talk.[1]

You could delete names entirely from most dialogue, but in some situations they're appropriate. A character should address another by name only with good reason to do so; for example, when characters meet.[2]

"Well, John Quincy, you old goat. I haven't seen you in ages."

Or when a character is trying to get another's attention.

"Franklin, would you give me a hand?"

Another is when the speaker is angry.[3]

"Michael John Klaassen, you stop that right now!"

Or when a character is in the heat of passion.[4]

Never mind. You get the idea.

CONTEXT

Sometimes the surrounding text makes it clear who is talking. Specifically, the lines preceding the line of dialogue can leave little doubt who is speaking.[5] For example,

Darin found Elsie in the garden. "Have I done something to offend you?"

An easy way to accomplish this is to put the character in action. If a character is doing something, and in that same paragraph he speaks, no one is confused about who is talking.

Henry bowed. "It's a pleasure to meet you."

Framing dialogue with action adds interest and helps avoid the problem where characters speak without engaging their surroundings, sometimes referred to as the "disembodied head" syndrome,[6] where the speakers seem to float in empty space. For example,

"May I have the honor of your next dance?"
"Sir, you may."
"I don't recall seeing you at Huntington before."
"I'm staying with my aunt and uncle for the summer."
"Mr. and Mrs. Ashcroft? They're my neighbors."

The opposite of the disembodied-head syndrome is the problem of hyperactive[7] characters, where a meaningless gesture accompanies each line of dialogue. For example,

Ashton sipped his champagne. "May I have the honor of your next dance?"
Liza handed her glass to a waiter. "Sir, you may."
Ashton scratched his chin. "I don't recall seeing you at Huntington before."
Liza brushed a stray lock of hair aside. "I'm staying with my aunt and uncle for the summer."
Ashton flicked a speck of lint from his sleeve. "Mr. and Mrs. Ashcroft? They're my neighbors."

Hyperactive characters are not just annoying; they bring attention to the author.

PARAGRAPHS

If a character other than the speaker is the subject of a sentence immediately preceding the dialogue, start a new paragraph for the dialogue. For example, the following is just fine.

Kenneth placed his hand on Maria's arm. "I love you."

Unless you meant to say,

Kenneth placed his hand on Maria's arm.
She said, "I love you."

The convention of starting a new paragraph whenever there is a new speaker is so widely accepted that if you begin a new paragraph with dialogue, the reader will assume the dialogue is spoken by a new speaker. This creates the potential for confusion if you start a new paragraph and don't intend to signal a new speaker. Who is the speaker in the second sentence below?

Kenneth placed his hand on Maria's arm.
"I love you."

Is Kenneth speaking or is Maria? When a character is the subject or speaker of the preceding paragraph, the reader will assume that a new paragraph signals a new speaker, unless you signal the reader otherwise.

As we have seen throughout this chapter, you have many ways to inform the reader who is speaking.

TAKEAWAYS

1. *Attributions* are words authors use to identify the speaker of dialogue.
2. When a character has a distinctive voice, no further help may be needed to identify the speaker.
3. *Direct address* refers to characters calling each other by name.
4. Characters should only address each other by name for good reason, such as when they meet, when trying to get each other's attention, and when the speaker is angry or in the heat of passion.
5. Context can make clear who is speaking.
6. One way to clarify who is talking is to precede dialogue with a sentence whose subject is the speaker of the dialogue.
7. *Disembodied head syndrome* refers to characters who speak without engaging their surroundings.
8. *Hyperactive characters* refers to dialogue in which each line of speech is accompanied by an all-but-meaningless gesture.
9. Start a paragraph for dialogue in which the subject of the previous sentence is a character other than the new speaker.

In the next chapter we'll address the verbs and adverbs of attribution.

11

VERBS AND ADVERBS OF ATTRIBUTION

CHAPTER CONTENTS
Verbs of attribution
Preferable attributions
Sometimes acceptable
Not acceptable
Adverbs of attribution
Prohibited adverbs in attributions
Potential exceptions
Alternatives

V erbs of *what?* Don't feel bad if you've never heard this term. I hadn't until I began the research for this book. A *verb of attribution* is that part of a *dialogue attribution* that shows how speech is uttered. For example, the verbs *said, whispered,* and *mumbled* are verbs of attribution. A verb of attribution together with a noun (or pronoun) forms an *attribution clause*. For example, the noun *Luke* together with the verb *shouted* becomes the attribution clause, as in,

Luke shouted, "Land ho!"

Verbs of attribution may be divided into three groups: preferable, acceptable, and unacceptable.

PREFERABLE

One word stands out as the most preferred verb of attribution, and that is *said*. Readers hardly notice it.

Said does its job so well that it's easy to overuse. Using *said* repeat-edly ~~can~~ create a staccato effect, especially in rapid-fire dialogue where each speaker makes a brief statement or asks a short question.

Rhonda said, "The party is tomorrow."
Agatha said, "I'm not going."
Rhonda said, "You're just being difficult."

Aspiring writers are taught is to avoid repetition, which can annoy the reader and create an impression that the writer is careless.[1] Overuse of the word *said* is largely a concern among writers, however, and not so much with readers.[2]

SOMETIMES ACCEPTABLE

Writers take pride in finding just the right word for each situation, and *said* is not the only acceptable verb of attribution. When a character is posing a question, the verb *asked* may be appropriate. If *asked* is okay, then why not *answered*? Sometimes a character needs to *whisper, mumble,* or *mutter, stammer,* or *stutter.* At other times he may feel compelled to *shout, yell,* or *scream.*

NOT ACCEPTABLE

Overuse of any word, even *said*, can become monotonous, but some substitutes are worse than repetition. In an attempt to avoid repeated use of the word *said*, some writers go to great lengths to find synonyms. Their characters *demand, insist, exclaim, explain, elaborate, state, mention, reply, respond, opine, retort, quiz, question, protest,* and *point out*. Such words are distracting. They show the writer attempting to be clever rather than letting the character's words and their context do the job.[3]

A further warning: some verbs used for dialogue attribution are physically impossible. Can humans really *bark* words? Or *hiss? Smile? Chuckle? Sigh? Whine? Groan?*

The all-time classic might be Herman Melville's whopper in *Moby-Dick*: "Ah! poor fellow! he'll have to die now," ejaculated the Long Island sailor.[4]

Rather than trying to find new and improved ways of saying *said*, focus on the words spoken by the character and the manner in which they are spoken.[5]

ADVERBS OF ATTRIBUTION

As with verbs of attribution, you may be tempted to get creative with adverbs. For example (adverbs in italics),

> "Sam is coming to the wedding," Bobbie said *archly*.
> Nancy said *snidely*, "You've got to be kidding."
> "You know," said Bobbie *sarcastically*, "I still love him."

Is there anything wrong with using adverbs in attribution clauses? Well, that depends. The subject of adverbs in dialogue attributions may be divided into three topics: prohibited, potential exceptions, and alternatives.

PROHIBITED ADVERBS IN ATTRIBUTIONS

A *verb*, including a verb of attribution such as *said*, describes an action. An *adverb* modifies or qualifies an action. Adverbs that modify verbs of attribution shift the reader's focus to the way something is said rather than on *what* is said. For example,

Riley said warmly, "You really know what you're doing."

The adverb *warmly* brings attention to itself, distracting the reader from what is said. Also as this example shows, adverbs tend to make dialogue sound awkward and unnatural. Rearranging the sentence magnifies the problem. For example,

"You really know what you're doing," Riley said warmly.

In this example the adverb comes at the end of the sentence, forcing the reader to backtrack to review how the sentence of dialogue was spoken, and that is never a good thing.

Never use an adverb to modify a verb of attribution.

POTENTIAL EXCEPTIONS

The prohibition of adverbs in attribution clauses has potential exceptions. You may be tempted to add an adverb where there may be confusion as to *how* words in dialogue are spoken. Or when you intend the words in dialogue to be spoken in a different manner than their apparent meaning.[6] For example,

"You badass!" she said admiringly.

Lilly said lovingly, "I just hate you."

Donna said proudly, "I gave that butthead the best years of my life."

As tempting as these potential exceptions may appear, they don't produce the best results, and they aren't necessary—which means they aren't exceptions after all, as the next section shows.

ALTERNATIVES

Readers should be able to figure out how the dialogue is delivered through context. What's the situation? What's the relationship between the characters? What's the personality of the characters? What words has the author chosen for the dialogue? Has the author described facial expressions, body language, or actions before the dialogue?

If dialogue and the surrounding text do their job, an adverb after the verb of attribution isn't necessary. And if dialogue and the surrounding text fail to do their jobs, adding an adverb compounds the problem by pointing out the shortfall.[7] Well-written dialogue tells the reader how it should be read.[8]

Rather than succumb to the siren call for adverbs that modify verbs of attribution, place a sentence before the dialogue that provides direction as to how the dialogue is to be read. That sentence may include the fiction-writing mode *action*. Using the examples from the previous section, consider the following.

She patted Henry on the back. "You badass!"

She smiled, caressed Sam's neck, and leaned close to him. "I just hate you."

Donna took a deep breath and smiled. "I gave that butthead the best years of my life."

In addition to action, the following fiction-writing modes may be helpful in providing direction as to how the dialogue should be read: introspection, recollection, sensation, or emotion. Consider the following.

Son of a gun, thought Jerry, this guy really does have some backbone. "You badass!"

Sheila recalled that Arthur had a sense of humor and liked to be teased. "I just hate you."

His hand strayed to where it shouldn't, and Kimberly felt her skin tingle. "You naughty boy."

She felt tears welling up. "I'm so happy."

Eliminating adverbs that modify verbs of attribution removes an unwelcome distraction for the reader and forces you to improve the dialogue so it stands on its own.

TAKEAWAYS

1. The preferred verb of attribution is *said*.
2. A handful of other verbs are sometimes acceptable.

3. Physically impossible verbs of attribution are not acceptable.
4. Never use an adverb to modify a verb of attribution.
5. Potential exceptions are not really exceptions because context can make clear what the speaker means.

In the next chapter we will explore how to use attributions to control rhythm and pace.

USING ATTRIBUTIONS TO CONTROL RHYTHM AND PACE

CHAPTER CONTENTS
Noun and verb order
Pronoun and verb order
Location
Selectivity
Long speeches
Inflection

S hould you use attributions even if the context makes it perfectly clear who's speaking? Should you try to eliminate all attributions? No. The primary purpose of attributions is to identify the speaker, but attributions also help control the rhythm and pace, or *flow*, of dialogue.

Attributions often consist of only two words (*he said*), so their use may appear to be simple. In reality, controlling rhythm and pace with dialogue tags involves a variety of issues: noun and verb order, pronoun and verb order, location, selectivity, long speeches, and inflection.

NOUN AND VERB ORDER

Which should you use? *Bob said* or *said Bob*? Certainly the former is more common than the latter. You've probably heard the admonition to always put the noun before an attribution verb (as in *Sam said*). You may have been taught that to put the verb in front of the noun (as in *said Sam*) sounds old-fashioned, corny, or awkward.

What difference does the order make if *said* is so invisible readers hardly notice it? Is this a distinction without a difference? Is this one of those issues writers fret about but readers don't even notice?

Rather than blindly following advice that may have questionable merit, let's look closer. First, does the location of the dialogue tag make a difference? How about if the tag is at the beginning of the sentence? For example, would you write the following?

> Said Billy, "Let's go to a movie."
> Said Donna, "I'd rather go to the symphony."

I would hope that your mind's ear and your writer's eye would make you wince at the awkwardness of such attributions compared with the following.

> Billy said, "Let's go to a movie."
> Donna said, "I'd rather go to the symphony."

Never place an attribution verb at the beginning of a sentence.

Let's look at other possibilities. For example,

> "Give me liberty, or give me death," Patrick Henry said.

Compared to

"Give me liberty, or give me death," said Patrick Henry.

To my ear "said Patrick Henry" at the end of the sentence sounds more natural than "Patrick Henry said." Others may disagree.

We've looked at attributions at the beginning of a sentence and at the end of a sentence, but what about in the middle?

"Give me liberty," Patrick Henry said, "or give me death."

"Give me liberty," said Patrick Henry, "or give me death."

Of these two examples, my preference is "said Patrick Henry," because to my ear the whole sentence sounds more natural and flows more smoothly. Others may prefer "Patrick Henry said." Neither is right, nor wrong. It's a personal preference, a matter of the writer's style, and an opportunity for variety.

Many writers advise placing the noun before the verb in attributions. To test my recommendations, I performed an informal survey of novels on my bookshelf. In a majority of the novels I sampled, the noun almost always preceded the verb. But in the following novels, the authors routinely placed *said* before the noun in attributions at the end of a sentence or in the middle:

- *To Kill a Mockingbird*, by Harper Lee
- *Holes*, by Louis Sachar
- *Ender's Game*, by Orson Scott Card
- *Eragon*, by Christopher Paolini
- *Harry Potter and the Sorcerer's Stone*, by J. K. Rowling

If the authors of these highly successful novels don't have a problem placing *said* before a noun at the end or middle of a sentence, neither should we.

PRONOUN AND VERB ORDER

Quite possibly the admonition to always place a *noun* before a verb of attribution spilled over from valid concerns about *pronoun*-verb order. Consider the following (pronouns in italics):

Said *he*, "The only thing we have to fear is fear itself."

"The only thing we have to fear," said *he*, "is fear itself."

"The only thing we have to fear is fear itself," said *he*.

I think Franklin D. Roosevelt would have agreed that "said he," "said she," and "said I" sound old-fashioned and contrived today, the literary equivalent of scratching fingernails across a chalkboard. Always place the pronoun before the verb in an attribution.

LOCATION

Which is the best place to put a dialogue tag? At the beginning of a sentence? The middle? The end? Let's consider attributions at the beginning of a sentence.

The woman said, "I'll take two of those."

Guido said, "Reach for the sky!"

The lookout yelled, "Land ho!"

To my ear, attributions at the beginning of a sentence are obtrusive to the point of distraction. Even worse is when several such sentences in a row begin with an attribution, as follows.

> Bob said, "I enjoyed the movie."
> Samantha said, "You've got to be kidding."
> Bob said, "I kid you not."

This treatment creates a script-like effect that is quite jarring to the reader. Place an attribution at the beginning of a sentence only if you want to draw extra attention to the speaker's identity—the equivalent of using a bullhorn.

Now let's look at attributions at the end of a sentence.

> "Romeo, Romeo. Wherefore, art thou, Romeo?" Juliet said.

> "Señorita, may I have the next dance?" asked Arturo.

> "You craven mortal, I curse you," Romulus said.

Attributions at the end of a sentence are common, but they can pose a big disadvantage: they force the reader to wait until the end of the sentence to find out who is speaking. The longer the sentence, the more it inconveniences the reader. In some cases, the reader may assume the wrong character is speaking until he gets to the attribution, and then he may have to read the dialogue again to get it right. Ugh!

What about dialogue tags in the middle of the sentence? Consider the following.

"Romeo, Romeo," said Juliet, "wherefore, art thou, Romeo?"

"Señorita," Arturo said, "may I have the next dance?"

"You craven mortal," said Romulus, "I curse you."

Obviously, an attribution in the middle of a sentence identifies the speaker earlier than one at the end of the sentence. It also creates opportunities to manipulate or improve rhythm and pace.

Dialogue tags placed in the middle of a sentence shouldn't be placed arbitrarily, though. For example, you wouldn't want something like:

"That is very strange, but I," said Lady Catherine, "suppose you had no opportunity."

Look for a natural pause, especially those marked with commas.[1] Then place the attribution where it contributes to the rhythm and pace of the passage. Use the placement of dialogue tags to influence how the sentence should be read.

"That is very strange," said Lady Catherine, "but I suppose you had no opportunity."

An attribution decreases the pace of dialogue slightly, so it may be used to slow important dialogue you don't want the reader to race through. Even when an attribution isn't necessary to tell us who's speaking, it may be needed to create a subtle pause in the conversation.

"Hey, guys," Samuel said with a chuckle, "it's the American way."

"You're ruining people's lives," said Archie, "and you brag about it?"

To slow the pace even further, replace the comma after the attribution with a period. For example.

"You craven mortal," Romulus said. "I curse you."

"That is very strange," said Lady Catherine. "But I suppose you had no opportunity."

Carefully select the location of your attributions to influence the rhythm and pace of dialogue.

SELECTIVITY

Even the most unobtrusive attribution shows the writer at work, and that is something to avoid when possible. Avoid using dialogue tags except when they are needed to identify the speaker or if they contribute to rhythm and pace.

The ultimate in an unobtrusive attribution, of course, is the one that isn't there—the attribution that has been omitted because the speaker's identity is clear.

In general, if a dialogue tag can be eliminated, you should leave it out. If the reader can tell who's talking, then a dialogue tag isn't necessary. Entire scenes between two people may be presented without attributions.

In some circumstances a speaker's identity may not be important. For example, in a highly emotional situation when several characters are talking simultaneously, attributions may not only be unnecessary, they may be distracting to the reader. Here's an example.

> After an eerie moment of silence, everyone started chattering.
> "This place gives me the jumpin' jitters."
> "Man, that was weird!"
> "Who spooked them?"
> "Where'd they go?"

The essence of deciding whether or not to use an attribution is balancing the desire to be unobtrusive with the need to control the rhythm and pace of the passage and the need to make sure the reader knows who is speaking.

LONG SPEECHES

Rambling monologues, long speeches, and lectures risk boring the reader. If a long passage of dialogue is necessary, break it up with incidental action or bits of introspection, recollection, emotion, or sensation to give the character (and the reader) a chance to catch his breath. A character shouldn't be allowed to ramble on like a windbag.

INFLECTION

Written fiction, including dialogue, is a form of silent communication.[2] As the author, you may use punctuation, word choice, and attributions to tell the reader how the dialogue should be read.

One of the most common writing tips is to read dialogue aloud, to hear the dialogue spoken. As with so many other tidbits of wisdom, this one shouldn't be followed blindly. Dialogue that is read aloud may include inflection that is not warranted by the written page.[3] A skillful orator can make clumsy writing sound better than it's written. A less skilled speaker of great dialogue may butcher it.

TAKEAWAYS

1. Even when attributions aren't needed to identify the speaker, they may be useful in controlling the rhythm and pace of dialogue.
2. Never place an attribution verb at the beginning of the sentence.
3. Trust your mind's ear when deciding whether to place the verb before the noun in attributions in the middle or at the end of a sentence.
4. Always place the pronoun before the verb in an attribution.
5. Place an attribution at the beginning of a sentence only if you want to draw extra attention to the identity of the speaker.
6. Avoid placing attributions at the end of long sentences.
7. When placing attributions in the middle of a sentence, insert them after a natural pause in the writing, such as after a comma.
8. The ultimate in unobtrusive attributions is the one that has been omitted because the identity of the speaker is clear.
9. Place attributions within a sentence to slow its pace.
10. In highly emotional situations where several people are speaking at once, dialogue tags may not be necessary.
11. Break up long speeches with incidental action or bits of introspection, recollection, emotion, or sensation.
12. Reading dialogue aloud may be counterproductive.

In the next chapter we'll explore ways to make dialogue sound natural.

13

MAKING DIALOGUE SOUND NATURAL

CHAPTER CONTENTS
Word choice
Unnecessary words
Profanity
Slang
Contractions
Sentences
Fragments
Grammar
Short sentences
Punctuation
Colloquialisms

S hould dialogue sound like everyday speech? If everyday speech were transcribed as dialogue, it would be annoying and boring—a torture to read. Real speech is filled with repetition, hesitation, interruption, verbalism, slang, regional or ethnic collo-quialisms, habitual words and phrases, and half-finished sentences.[1] [2]

So if replicating actual speech in fiction is undesirable, how should dialogue be structured to make it sound natural? Dialogue intended to create the impression of real conversation must strike a balance between artifice and documentary replication of spontaneous speech.[3]

Fictional dialogue should come across as unique and interesting. Compared to real life, it's more charming, fresh, intelligent, clever, and better argued.[4] Even characters that aren't bigger than life need to be at their best when they speak. Fictional characters can say the things we wish we would have said if we had time to think our words through in advance.

Compared to real-world speech, fictional dialogue is compressed, shaped, understated, or emphasized.[5] Dialogue is compressed by eliminating unnecessary words. It's shaped through planning for clarity and purpose. And it may be either understated or emphasized to meet the story's needs, including characterization.

Dialogue is made to *sound* realistic on several levels: words, sentences, punctuation, and colloquialisms.

WORD CHOICE

As with any writing, effective dialogue begins with selecting the most appropriate, precise, apt word for any particular situation. For example, the words *lie, mislead,* and *obfuscate* can mean the same thing, but one may be the most realistic, depending upon the character and the situation. For example,

"You lie!"
"Your statement is misleading."
"Your testimony appears to intentionally obfuscate the facts of the situation."

To which of the following characters would you assign each of the above statements?

- A judge pronouncing a prison sentence upon a felon.
- A reporter conducting an interview.
- A woman confronting a cheating boyfriend.

UNNECESSARY WORDS

Real-life conversation includes unnecessary words such as *no, oh, well,* and *like.* Also included may be unnecessary chitchat or repetition. Try to eliminate unnecessary words from dialogue. Here's an example of what a real-life conversation might sound like.

"Hey, buddy, what's up?"

"Oh, nothing much. How about you?"

"Just trying to stay out of trouble. Uh, I've got a favor to ask."

"Sure, anything for you, pal. What do you need?"

"Well, this is a little awkward, but could you come over to my place, like right now?"

Realistic fictional dialogue might be more like this:

"Hey, Pete, could you come to my place right now?"

PROFANITY

For some people, everyday speech is peppered with profanity. Such words may be a liability in fictional dialogue, even if you think it is appropriate to a character and the situation. You need to consider the target audience, especially if you intend to market the book commercially, because profanity may prove a hurdle. A little profanity goes a long way. Use profanity only in story situations where a strong, possibly shocking, word is needed.

Writers make lots of decisions, and writers of all types of fiction are faced with hard choices regarding profanity. Like it or not, the use of profanity is an effective device for portraying emotion in fiction, adding realism to dialogue and to a character's introspection. So how do writers balance the desire for authenticity with the need to be responsible? The choices come down to (1) liberal use of profanity, (2) omission of profanity, (3) sparse use of profanity, (4) summarized profanity, and (5) sanitized profanity.

Liberal Use of Profanity. In some ways, this is the easiest of the choices. Rather than agonize about the use of foul language in novels, writers may just use it wherever it seems natural. After all, nearly everyone has heard and read foul language before, and it's been decades since it's been taboo in fiction.

On the other hand, there are serious drawbacks to the liberal use of profanity. First of all, if a writer needs profanity to make dialogue seem realistic, then a *lot* of it may be needed. For any work of fiction, overuse of profanity can become an annoying distraction to the reader. For some readers, it's an outright turnoff, leading them to promptly put the book down.

For some fiction, there's a substantial economic price to pay for the use of profanity. Although most readers purchase their own reading material, buyers of teen novels are often parents, grandparents, teachers, and librarians. Many adults are reluctant to purchase teen fiction that includes gratuitous use of profanity. Editors, publishers, and book reviewers, both professional and on Amazon, may share those feelings.

Omission of Profanity. An alternative to the liberal use of profanity is to avoid the issue by totally leaving it out of your manuscript. After all, the best of fictional dialogue isn't a transcription of real-life conversation: it's distilled down to the very best and most appropriate, given the needs of the story.

If the characters and dialogue in the story are believable without profanity, there's no problem. But will all of the characters be believable if they never use profanity, even in situations where its use seems natural? Maybe a compromise is in order.

Sparse Use of Profanity. Why not use profanity only in those few situations that are most important to the story? This approach has a benefit: If you seldom use profanity in your writing, it will have more impact when you actually do.

Summarized Use of Profanity. If you're trying to limit or avoid the outright use of foul language, but the needs of the story call for it, the use of summary may be an acceptable alternative. *Summarized profanity* means using phrases like "he cussed," "she cursed," and "he cut loose with a string of expletives." In fact, summary may very well serve the story better than interrupting the action with dialogue or distracting the reader with specific curse words.

Sanitized Profanity. By *sanitized*, I mean sugar-coated substitutes. "Fiddle-dee-dee," might be fine for Scarlet O'Hara in *Gone with the Wind*. And "Oh, fudge!" "Shoot!" and "Darn it!" could be appropriate for some characters. On the other hand, there are situations where the words *manure*, *dung*, or *poop* might not adequately communicate a particular character's emotion.

My young-adult novels deal with troubled teens, boys likely to pepper their conversation with expletives. As a novelist, I've weighed the costs and benefits of using profanity and have developed my personal guidelines:

- The younger the intended reader, the harder it is to justify using any profanity at all.
- I won't use liberal amounts of profanity in my writing; in fact, I'll use profanity only reluctantly where I believe the benefit outweighs the cost.
- I'll use sanitized cursing where appropriate and summarized profanity where it serves the story best.

SLANG

Especially for some groups of people, real speech is filled with trendy expressions, slang, and colloquialisms.[6] Much like profanity, slang is a double-edged sword. Slang can help make dialogue sound realistic in contemporary fiction. Slang tends to be specific to a timeframe or a region, so including expressions appropriate to historic fiction or genre fiction can add verisimilitude. In our rapidly changing world, even fiction meant to be contemporary today may shortly become historical fiction set in the not-so-distant past. On the other hand, the popularity of trendy words often fades fast, so what's trendy today may seem outdated, out of touch, or awkward before your story is ready for publication,[7] or shortly thereafter, limiting its appeal.

CONTRACTIONS

One of the simplest ways to make dialogue seem natural is to use contractions. If a character is coming across as stiff—whether she's overly formal, uncomfortable in social situations, or has a rigid personality—then use more contractions.[8]

Unless in a state of high emotion ("You are a liar!"), people tend to speak in contractions. More than likely *you* use contractions in your everyday speech, and so should your characters.[9]

SENTENCES

In real life, some people speak in short, clipped sentences while others ramble. The length of a character's dialogue can indicate the person's power over listeners. People who hold the floor for a long time without interruption may have status, while those not permitted to speak or speak for long may have less influence. Others who talk a lot are merely bores.

Dialogue in fiction needs to be concise to avoid driving the reader nuts. So how do you portray longwinded characters? Either by summarizing their windiness or by cutting them off. Here's an example of a summarized conversation. Note how the omitted dialogue is shown as an ellipsis.

> "The Bengal tiger is a fascinating creature. After decades of military service in India, I can enlighten you about..."
> Reggie stifled a yawn and fought to stay awake as the colonel droned on for another fifteen minutes.

Here's an example of cutting off the same character. Note how the cut-off dialogue ends with an em dash.

> "The Bengal tiger is a fascinating creature. After decades of military service in India, I can enlighten you about—"
> "Yes, yes, Colonel," said Reggie, "no doubt we all want to hear more about tigers and look forward to joining you in the parlor after dinner. But first, we must thank our hosts for their hospitality."

FRAGMENTS

In dialogue, sentence fragments are useful in conveying natural-sounding speech. "Makes sense?"

GRAMMAR

Dialogue doesn't require all the formalities of grammar or sentence structure. We should try to use perfect grammar when we write, but we usually don't when we talk.[10] Of course, having a character speak with perfect grammar tells us some thing about that individual's personality. Dialogue needs to sound natural, so you should allow for leeway in grammar and sentence structure in dialogue.

SHORT SENTENCES

The use of short sentences is acceptable in dialogue. "You see?"

PUNCTUATION

Punctuation in dialogue should be kept simple[11] and less formal than in other writing. Never use colons or semicolons in dialogue. Avoid overusing punctuation marks that stand out in print, such as ellipses and dashes.

COLLOQUIALISMS

Back in the time of Mark Twain and Joel Chandler Harris (the Uncle Remus stories), authors intentionally tried to duplicate dialect in dialogue for the sake of authenticity. They used contractions and elisions, and they purposely misspelled words in an attempt to replicate regional and ethnic dialect and pronunciation. For example,

"Hey mon, gotta gitcha some dat punkin pii."

I find this type of dialogue difficult to read and annoying. When you want to portray dialect, use a few carefully selected words, elisions, and contractions to indicate pronunciation and cadence, and then trust your reader to "hear" your character correctly. For example,

"Hey man, you gotta get some of that punkin pie."

Another technique for handling dialect is simply to state that the speaker has an accent. For example:

Bubba spoke with an Oklahoma twang. "It's just up the road a piece."

TAKEAWAYS

1. To make dialogue seem more natural, avoid creating dialogue that sounds too realistic.
2. Compared to real-world speech, fictional dialogue is compressed, shaped, understated, or emphasized.
3. Effective dialogue begins with selecting the most appropriate, precise, apt word for any particular situation.
4. Eliminate unnecessary words.
5. The younger the intended reader, the harder it is to justify using profanity.
6. Use profanity only where you believe the benefits outweigh the costs.

7. Use sanitized or summarized profanity where it serves the story best.
8. Slang may help make dialogue sound natural, but slang that is contemporary at the time of writing may be obsolete by publication, limiting your work's shelf life.
9. Use contractions to help make dialogue sound more natural.
10. Match sentence length to the character and the circumstances.
11. Don't let characters ramble.
12. Sentence fragments may help create natural-sounding dialogue.
13. Dialogue doesn't require all the formalities of grammar or sentence structure.
14. Short sentences are acceptable.
15. Keep punctuation in dialogue simple.
16. Avoid trying to replicate colloquial speech.

In the next chapter we will cover the mechanics of punctuating dialogue.

PUNCTUATING DIALOGUE

CHAPTER CONTENTS
Punctuation
Quotation marks
Paragraphs
Exclamation points
Question marks
Colons and semicolons
Dashes
Ellipses
Numbers and dates
Italics
Font changes

Conversation is the most easily recognized of the fiction-writing modes because of its punctuation. Of all the fiction-writing modes, dialogue has the most specialized issues regarding punctuation and formatting, including quotation marks, paragraphs, exclamation points, question marks, colons, semicolons, dashes, ellipses, numbers, dates, and font changes.

QUOTATION MARKS

No fiction-writing mode is more closely tied to a specific punctuation mark than dialogue is to the quotation mark. The mechanics of quotation marks for dialogue are specific. A character's spoken words are enclosed in quotation marks, for example,

> "My, Granny, what a big mouth you have."

Note that the period is inside the closing quotation mark.

Often dialogue includes words to tell the reader which character is speaking, an *attribution* or a *dialogue tag*. If the attribution precedes the dialogue, separate the tag from the quote with a comma.

> Little Red Riding Hood said, "My, Granny, what a big mouth you have."

If a dialogue tag falls within the quote, frame it with commas.

> "My, Granny," said Little Red Riding Hood, "what a big mouth you have."

If an attribution tag falls after the quote, place a comma within the closing quotation mark.

> "My, Granny, what a big mouth you have," said Little Red Riding Hood.

If an attribution tag falls after the quote, and an exclamation point or a question mark terminates the quote, place it inside the closing quotation mark:

"My, Granny, what a big mouth you have!" said Little Red Riding Hood.

Use double quotation marks, as in the examples above, when your character is speaking his own words. If your character is quoting someone else, enclose the other person's words with single quotes. For example,

Linda stood in front of the class and recited, "Little Red Riding Hood said, 'My, Granny, what a big mouth you have.'"

If your character is only summarizing another's words (not quoting the exact words), no single quotation marks are needed.

Little Red Riding Hood commented on the size of her grandmother's mouth.

PARAGRAPHS

Whenever a different character begins to talk, indicate the change of speaker with a new paragraph. This rule may be carried too far. If a paragraph is already focused on a character, then including dialogue by that same character is acceptable, even preferred. For example,

Tom figured the scientist was wasting his time, but it didn't hurt to humor him. "Shootin' for a Nobel prize or something?"

In the above example, it is clear who is doing the speaking.

Starting a new paragraph for dialogue by the character who is the focus of the previous sentence risks confusing the reader, because he will assume that a new paragraph signals that a different character is speaking. For example,

> Tom figured the scientist was wasting his time, but it didn't hurt to humor him.
> "Shootin' for a Nobel prize or something?"

In the above example, the reader would understandably assume the dialogue is spoken by someone other than Tom.

What if a speaker gabs for more than one paragraph? The signal to the reader that the same speaker is beginning a new paragraph is to *not* close the quotes at the end of the first paragraph(s). Here's an example from a speech by General Andrew Jackson in New Orleans during the War of 1812.

> "Are we the titled slaves of George the third? The military conscripts of Napoleon the Great? Or the frozen peasants of the Russian Czar? I say no. We are the freeborn sons of America. The citizens of the only republic now existing in the world. And the only people on earth who possess rights, liberties, and property which they dare call their own.
> "Good Citizens, you must all rally around me in this emergency. Cease all differences and unite with me in patriotic resolve to save this city from dishonor and disaster which a presumptuous enemy threatens to inflict upon it."

Omission of an ending quote from a paragraph in a multiparagraph quote is an established convention, but it's also easy to miss. The risk is that the reader might need to backtrack to figure out who is doing the speaking (never a good thing). A better technique is to close the quote at the end of the paragraph, then break up the long speech by beginning the next paragraph with incidental action that reminds the reader who is talking. For example (see incidental action in italics),

"Are we the titled slaves of George the third? The military conscripts of Napoleon the Great? Or the frozen peasants of the Russian Czar? I say no. We are the freeborn sons of America. The citizens of the only republic now existing in the world. And the only people on earth who possess rights, liberties, and property which they dare call their own."

Jackson gripped the ornamental railing and leaned toward the crowd. "Good Citizens, you must all rally around me in this emergency. Cease all differences and unite with me in patriotic resolve to save this city from dishonor and disaster which a presumptuous enemy threatens to inflict upon it."

An alternative to using incidental action in the above example would be to use an attribution such as *Jackson continued.*

EXCLAMATION POINTS

Exclamation points are acceptable punctuation marks in dialogue, but too many of them dilute their impact. Their use may be an attempt to spice up bland writing. A better solution is to strive for writing that is effective without the use of an exclamation point as a crutch. For example, consider the following.

"Reach for the sky!"

There is nothing grammatically wrong with this dialogue, but it could be more effective if restructured as:

Bogart pulled his pistol. "Reach for the sky."

Here, action dramatizes the line, making an exclamation point unnecessary, even melodramatic. The dialogue itself and the surrounding text should make clear how dialogue is delivered, rendering most exclamation marks unnecessary.

Using *said* after an exclamation point diminishes the exclamation point. For example,

"You're a real jerk!" said Rachel.

Along the same line, using *shouted*, *screamed*, or *yelled* after an exclamation point seems redundant. For example,

"Zombies!" shouted Winnie.

If the speaker needs to be identified, maybe another technique could be used, such as preceding the dialogue with incidental action. For example,

Daisy clenched her fist. "Them's fightin' words."

Here, it is clear who is speaking, and the exclamation point is unnecessary.

QUESTION MARKS

The use of question marks is fairly straightforward. Once again, the mark usually goes inside the final quotation mark, as in:

"Do you love me, or not?"

Adding "asked" or "questioned" afterward is redundant, as in:

"Do you love me, or not?" asked Christine.

If the speaker needs to be identified, another technique could be used.

Christine sneered. "Do you love me, or not?"

COLONS AND SEMICOLONS

Colons and semicolons are unusual within dialogue, and for good reason. They add little to dialogue and run the risk of looking odd and out of place. Colons and semicolons provide clues that are not auditory. Dialogue is heard, not seen. Never use colons or semicolons in dialogue. In dialogue, an em dash may often be substituted for a semicolon.

DASHES

An *em dash* gets its name by being as wide as a printed upper-case M. An em dash may be used to show interrupted speech. For example,

"I'll see you later after I—"
"The sky is falling!"

ELLIPSES

Specialized rules exist for ellipses in dialogue. Ellipses, also known as ellipsis points, show an omission of words or letters. As a punctuation device, "an ellipsis is a series of three dots."[1]

In dialogue, ellipses signal two situations: (1) the speaker's utterance is not completed, and (2) a pause in the speaker's utterance.

Here's an example of an utterance not brought to completion.

The witch said, "Step into my cottage and..."

No additional period is added as terminal punctuation, and "no space intervenes between a final ellipsis point and a closing quotation mark."[2]

Here's an example showing pauses in the speaker's utterance.

"You're not...really...? Because if you are...," she said. "I have a hard time, you know.... Oh, my, I'm.... This is so incredibly...!"

For clarity or ease of reading, the three dots may be preceded or followed (depending upon where the omission occurs) by a period, a comma, a question mark, or an exclamation point. "The first word after an ellipsis is capitalized if it begins a new grammatical sentence."[3]

NUMBERS

In general, regarding numbers in dialogue, spell out whole numbers from zero through one hundred.[4] Likewise, for whole numbers one through one hundred followed by *hundred, thousand,* or *hundred thousand.*[5] For example,

- two
- ten
- nineteen
- ninety-six

- twenty-first century
- 1970s
- eight hundred
- six thousand
- fifty thousand
- three hundred thousand
- forty-two million
- 101
- 453
- 7,777
- 33,555,300

"When a number begins a sentence, it is always spelled out, [but] a sentence can often be recast."[6] For example,

"One hundred fifty-one applied for the job."
"In total, 151 applied for the job."

Exceptions to the general rule apply to dates, large numbers, physical quantities, money, etc., so you may want to consult *The Chicago Manual of Style*[7] for specifics.

ITALICS

To add emphasis to dialogue, use italics. For example,

"Do you *really* want to jump off that cliff?"
"I don't really want to jump off a cliff, but I'm willing to jump for *you*."

The purpose of using italics is to emphasize a word (or at most a phrase or sentence). Avoid using italics for more than a few words. A whole block of dialogue in italics would be distracting.

Another use for italics is to highlight terms defined in the same sentence. For example,

> "A *bateau*," said Samuel, "is a flat-bottomed boat with a pointed bow and stern."

Once the term is defined, no italics are used in subsequent uses of that word.

Occasionally writers use italics to indicate a voice heard only by the viewpoint character.[8] For example,

> A ghost appeared at the top of the stairs, and Morris felt, rather than heard, the warning, *Proceed no farther.*

FONT CHANGES

Another technique used by some writers is to change the print font as a means of signaling a transition. Font changes distract and annoy the reader. Avoid font changes in fiction.

There may always be writers who intentionally break conventions for the purpose of stylistic experimentation. Innovation has its place. For the most part, however, writers who fail to abide by the specialized conventions of dialogue punctuation risk annoying or confusing their readers.

TAKEAWAYS

1. Follow the rules for using quotation marks in dialogue.
2. Indicate a change of speaker with a new paragraph.
3. When a paragraph is already focused on one character, a new paragraph is not needed if that character speaks.

4. Omission of ending quotation marks in a multiparagraph quote is an established convention, but this practice risks confusing the reader if the next paragraph doesn't promptly indicate who is speaking.

5. Dialogue itself and the surrounding text should indicate how dialogue is delivered, rendering most exclamation points unnecessary.

6. Adding "asked" or "questioned" after a question mark is redundant.

7. Never use colons or semicolons in dialogue.

8. Use an em dash to show interrupted speech.

9. Ellipses show an omission of words or a pause in speech.

10. Numbers zero through one hundred should be spelled out.

11. Italics may be used to add emphasis to dialogue.

12. Italics are also used to highlight terms defined in the same sentence.

13. Avoid font changes in fiction.

This chapter concludes our exploration of dialogue. Next, we'll examine the mode of narration in ways you may not have considered.

PART IV

EXTERIORITY

Four fiction-writing modes may be classified as *exteriority* since they represent what is outside your character's mind: narration, description, exposition, and transition.

15

NARRATION

The fiction-writing mode that communicates directly with the reader.

CHAPTER CONTENTS
Obtrusive narration
Unobtrusive narration
Disguised narration

N*arration* is the fiction-writing mode whereby the narrator communicates directly to the reader. Narration comes in three types: obtrusive, unobtrusive, and disguised.

OBTRUSIVE NARRATION

In *obtrusive narration* the narrator conspicuously communicates with the reader, a technique not commonly used today, although it was popular in the 1800s and before. Obtrusive narration comes in three forms: direct-address, reminder, and forecasting.

All three forms of obtrusive narration are outdated techniques little used in modern fiction, and for good reason: they're an annoying reminder that an author is narrating rather than letting the reader "live" the story. Each form of obtrusive narration is described here to enable you to recognize them in the writing of others and, I hope, avoid them in your own writing.

In *direct address* the narrator names the reader. For example,

> Now, dear reader, we shall learn the plight of darling Polly, who...

Reminder narration helps the reader recall what previously transpired in the story.

> Some chapters back, you may recall, Robin Hood encountered Little John and defeated him.

Forecasting narration alerts the reader to what may lie ahead in the story.

> Little did King Arthur know that he would soon be...

UNOBTRUSIVE NARRATION

Unobtrusive narration is also direct communication from the narrator to the reader, but it lacks the blatancy of direct address. Whatever observation the author wants to communicate to the reader is simply stated without any attempt to channel it through a viewpoint character. For example,

> A copper-colored, wormlike creature wriggled across the floor.

Here's another:

> If the rumors were accurate, they would be meeting Indians recruited by the great Shawnee leader Tecumseh.

In both of these examples, as presented without any context, the narrator communicates directly to the reader without filtering the observation through a character.

DISGUISED NARRATION

Disguised narration differs from unobtrusive narration in that it flows through the viewpoint of a character and is thus converted into one of the other fiction-writing modes. Consider the following revision of the first example under unobtrusive narration.

> Bodie watched as a copper-colored, wormlike creature wriggled across the floor.

Here, the narration is still present, word for word, but since the phrase *Bodie watched as* precedes the narration, the reader can imagine "seeing" the creature from the viewpoint of the character. The narrative has been disguised as, or converted to, the fiction-writing mode *sensation*.

Now consider a revision of the second example of unobtrusive narration.

> Relaxing a little, Lemuel thought about the coming day. If the rumors were accurate, they would be meeting Indians recruited by the great Shawnee leader Tecumseh.

Here, the narrative is preceded by a *sentence* that is clearly through the viewpoint of the character. The reader can imagine the subsequent sentence as "thinking" through the mind of the character, thus disguising the narrative as introspection.

Is it necessary to use a thinking, feeling, or sensing verb (sometimes referred to as a *filter verb*) to disguise narrative? Not always. A sentence with the viewpoint character as the *subject* may suffice. For example,

> Bodie froze. A copper-colored, wormlike creature wriggled across the floor.

And,

> Lemuel relaxed a little. If the rumors were accurate, they would be meeting Indians recruited by the great Shawnee leader Tecumseh.

The introductory sentences above use the viewpoint character as the subject of the sentence, implying that the viewpoint is that of the character, especially if that character's viewpoint was established in earlier passages. After an introductory sentence, the following text can thus be imagined by the reader as flowing through the mind of the character, disguising the narrative as another fiction-writing mode.

Once the viewpoint character is established, the narrative can continue for sentences, even paragraphs, without using such a "filter" verb. For example:

> Bodie froze. A copper-colored, wormlike creature wriggled across the floor. The creepy, three-inch bug's tiny legs

blurred with motion as it skittered toward a crack in the cave wall.

And,

> Relaxing a little, Lemuel thought about the coming day. If the rumors were accurate, they would be meeting Indians recruited by the great Shawnee leader Tecumseh. He had been encouraging tribes from the Great Lakes all the way down to the Gulf of Mexico to unite and halt American acquisition of native lands. In recent months, thousands of Indians had gathered near the confluence of the Wabash and Tippecanoe rivers. The village, named Prophet's Town after the chief's brother, was to be the capital of the new Indian confederation.

Even longer passages of narration may be converted to another fiction-writing mode by strategically inserting thinking, feeling, or sensing verbs or sentences with the viewpoint character as the subject. For example, see "thought Bodie" (in italics) in the following:

> Bodie froze. A copper-colored, wormlike creature wriggled across the floor. The creepy, three-inch bug's tiny legs blurred with motion as it skittered toward a crack in the cave wall. A centipede or a millipede, *thought Bodie*, wondering how to tell the difference.

Even though all written fiction is narrated, and thus has a narrator,[1] some stories, even entire novels, have no *apparent* narrator. Some authors choose to camouflage narration, to make the narrator so unobtrusive that the narrator never addresses the reader directly. Instead of direct address, the author presents the entire story through a viewpoint character, converting narration to other fiction-writing modes that flow through the mind of the viewpoint character (introspection, sensation, emotion, or recollection), where that character thinks, hears, sees, smells, feels, or recalls whatever the narrator decides to communicate.

TAKEAWAYS

1. Narration comes in three forms: obtrusive, unobtrusive, and disguised.
2. Avoid obtrusive narration in all its forms.
3. Rather than narrating obtrusively or unobtrusively, disguise narrated material as another fiction mode.
4. To convert narration to another fiction-writing mode, write the material as if it is being perceived by the viewpoint character.
5. By disguising narration as another fiction-writing mode, entire stories may be written with no apparent narrator.

In the next chapter we'll look at the challenges, pitfalls, and opportunities of bringing fiction to life with description.

DESCRIPTION

The fiction-writing mode that portrays people, places, things, or
concepts.

CHAPTER CONTENTS
Vividness
Word choice
Details
Nouns: concrete vs. abstract
Nouns: specific vs. general
Nouns: singular vs. plural
Denotation vs. connotation
Conciseness
Syntax
Figures of speech
Spatial organization
Clarity
Quantity
Obtrusiveness

Description is the fiction-writing mode for transmitting a mental image of the particulars of a story, including characters, plot, and setting. It adds depth and at its best causes the reader to have an emotional experience, bringing fiction to life.

The degree to which description brings life to a story is *vividness*.[1] Fortunately, writers have numerous tools with which to create effective description:

- Word choice
- Details
- Nouns: concrete vs. abstract, specific vs. general, and singular vs. plural
- Denotation vs. connotation
- Conciseness

WORD CHOICE

The foundation of description is word choice. To find the right word is to find the word best suited to the task, the word that matches the image the writer desires, the word that evokes the emotion the writer intends.

The right word has little or no chance of being confused with another meaning. "The difference between the right word and the almost right word," according to Mark Twain, "is the difference between lightning and the lightning bug."[2]

DETAILS

Details can add depth and credibility to description. Unfortunately, in an attempt to create description that appears real, writers may be tempted to include too many details. So as not to overburden description, you need to decide *which* details to include. Details range in importance from irrelevant to vital.

Not everything needs to be described. If something is implied, it doesn't need to be portrayed in detail.[3] For example, in describing an elephant, do you really need to mention that it is huge, gray, has floppy ears, a long, flexible trunk, and ivory tusks? All of this description is understood at the mention of the word *elephant*.

On the other hand, if the reader is not likely to be familiar with the thing being portrayed, then more details may be warranted. If the story features a wombat instead of an elephant, at least some description of a wombat is appropriate.

The most vital details are *telling*. With a minimal number of words, they reveal the essence of the image. For example, the writer may accomplish his objective by describing a character as wearing a bikini. A string bikini might be adequate, but how about a black string bikini? Or a black string bikini top stretched so tight it might burst? What if the bikini is made of clear plastic? Alligator hide? A single telling detail can radically change a vague image to one that evokes emotional uniqueness, individuality, or meaning.

NOUNS: CONCRETE VS. ABSTRACT

What do the words *desk, robin,* and *tractor* have in common versus *humor, fear,* and *sanity*? The first three words refer to something physical and are *concrete nouns*. The second three words are *abstract nouns,* referring to intangibles.

A concrete noun triggers a mental image. For example, when you read the word *engine*, a mental image probably pops into your mind. Abstract nouns don't generate such images. For example, if you read *ingenuity*, what do you picture? Probably nothing.

Here's an example of description using abstract nouns (determination, adversary, combat).

> With determination, Shane engaged his adversary in combat.

Here's an example of description using concrete nouns (sword, stroke, musket, bayonet, redcoat, chest).

> Shane parried the sword stroke with his musket, then thrust his bayonet into the redcoat's chest.

Both concrete and abstract nouns have a role in fiction, but concrete nouns help create vivid description.

NOUNS: SPECIFIC VS. GENERAL

Nouns may be specific (or particular), or they may be general (or vague). *Specific* nouns create robust description. Unless the needs of the story favor the use of a general noun, try to be specific. Instead of describing an automobile as *a car* (general and vague), describe it as a *Mercedes 450SL convertible* (specific and particular).

Specifics enhance description, but adding specifics just for the sake of doing so is a wasted opportunity to improve the story. For example, describing an auto as a purple VW bug creates an entirely different image than a Mercedes, but why does that matter to the story? What does driving a VW instead of a Mercedes tell you about the character? What role does the vehicle play in the plot? Why is the VW purple? Specificity in description is desirable, but make sure it enhances the story. Otherwise, it's distracting clutter.

NOUNS: SINGULAR VS. PLURAL

Singular nouns create different images than do plural nouns. For example, *cow*, *calf*, *bull*, and *steer* generate specific images that vary from those created by the word *cattle*. And *goose* generates an entirely different image than do the words *geese*, *gaggle*, or *flock*. The nature of the story often dictates the use of either a singular or a plural noun, but sometimes you have a choice, and that choice can make a world of difference in the image evoked.

DENOTATION VS. CONNOTATION

Words sometimes have more than one meaning. *Denotation* refers to the literal meaning of a word.[4] *Connotation* refers to how people feel about the word: an implied or suggested meaning.[5] For example, a *snake* is a reptile, but the word may also refer to someone who is untrustworthy. The word *slim* implies health and attractiveness, but *skinny* has negative connotations.

When writing description be mindful of denotation versus connotation. Would you describe your character as a security consultant, a freedom fighter, a hired gun, a defense contractor, a soldier of fortune, or a mercenary? Was your character swayed, convinced, persuaded, or brainwashed? Connotation provides an opportunity to add depth or humor to your fiction.

CONCISENESS

Finding the right word is important, but so is elimination of unnecessary words. Unnecessary words dilute description, making it less effective. They can slow the process of reading, even to the point that the reader doesn't finish the story. Unnecessary words come in many forms: redundancies, expletives, modifiers, and doubles of almost anything.

Redundancies can slip into description anywhere. For example, *The redcoats retreated back to the trees.* Here, *retreated back* is a tautology, as the word *retreat* is synonymous with backward movement.

Among the least necessary adverbs and adjectives are the redundant modifiers. For example, *Many married couples owed their initial meeting to Mrs. Madison.* Here, the word *initial* is unnecessary, as the context indicates that the couples met for the first time.

Also consider: *Hawkeye grabbed the axe and chopped vigorously.* The verb *chopped* implies with vigor: swinging an axe without vigor would not be chopping, so the adverb *vigorously* is redundant and unnecessary.

An *intensifier* is a modifier that amplifies the meaning of the word it modifies.[6] Examples include *very, quite, extremely, highly,* and *greatly,* as in *His Majesty King George III was a much-maligned monarch, greatly misunderstood but also quite ineffective.*

Just the opposite of an intensifier is a *qualifier,* a modifier that weakens the word modified.[7] Examples include *fairly, somewhat, rather,* and *barely,* as in *His Majesty King George III was a fairly ineffective monarch, somewhat misunderstood, and sometimes maligned.*

Intensifiers and qualifiers lack the primary characteristic of adverbs: the ability to modify verbs.[8] Intensifiers modify only adjectives and adverbs. Intensifiers and qualifiers diminish the effectiveness and immediacy of writing.

Rather than use an intensifier or a qualifier, use a more specific word. For example, instead of *an extremely large dog* write *a huge dog.* Instead of a *very small poodle* write a *tiny poodle.* Intensifiers and qualifiers may not be needed at all, as in *His Majesty King George III was an ineffective monarch, misunderstood and maligned.*

Expletives may be classified into three categories: syntactic expletives, expletive attributives, and bad language.[9] *Syntactic expletives* are filler words adding nothing to a sentence.[10] Examples include *it* and *there* when used as a dummy subject, as in *It is hot today,* or *There will come a time for revenge.*

Expletive attributives are modifiers that contribute little to the meaning of the sentence.[11] An expletive attributive may suggest strength of feeling (anger, irritation, admiration) and thus become a grammatical intensifier. For example, *damn, bloody,* and *wretched,* as in:

> They disconnected the damned phone.
> We better get our bloody act together.
> He had to obey the wretched order.

The word *expletive* is also commonly used to describe vulgar, obscene, or profane language, much of which contributes little if anything to description.

Another opportunity for conciseness lies in the elimination of double words. In an effort to be accurate, you may be tempted to use two words (nouns, verbs, prepositions, modifiers) where one would suffice. Sometimes two words are needed, but often they are not, meaning one of the words is redundant.

Consider the following examples.

> Jill hopped and skipped down the hill.
> Bodie reached out over the ledge.
> Lemuel slowly and carefully raised his rifle
> Rachel washed the dirty and greasy pan.

Evan outlined his goals and objectives for the year.

Are *hopped* and *skipped* both necessary to describe Jill's action? Do you really need both *out* and *over* to describe reaching? Wouldn't *carefully* imply *slowly* reaching for a rifle? A dirty pan may not be greasy, but a greasy pan will be dirty. Aren't *goals* and *objectives* the same thing?

Sometimes the context and your intent require two words for adequate description, but often one word will do the job. Better to pick the most appropriate word, and let it stand on its own.

> Jill skipped down the hill.
> Bodie reached over the ledge.
> Lemuel carefully raised his rifle
> Rachel washed the dirty pan.
> Evian outlined his goals for the year.

Unnecessary words dilute writing and make it less effective.

Other factors contribute to bringing description to life: syntax, figures of speech, spatial organization, clarity, quantity, and obtrusiveness.

SYNTAX

A fundamental function of a writer is to organize words and phrases into sentences. The orderly arrangement of words is called *syntax*. Words may be organized into sentences in many ways, each with different emphasis and varying degrees of grace. For example:

> Beyond the shoreline rose a steep clay bank.
> Beneath the steep clay bank lay the shoreline.

Above the shoreline rose a steep bank of clay.

As these examples demonstrate, changes in syntax create variation in meaning and emphasis.

The examples also show that the word in a sentence most remembered by a reader is the last. Stated differently, the last word of a sentence is the most remembered. Just as different words may be selected to create a desired effect, syntax may be manipulated to fit the needs of the situation.

FIGURES OF SPEECH

Literary devices called *figures of speech* may enrich description. Figures of speech include various techniques in which words are used in other than their usual manner to suggest an image, emotion, sensation, tone, or other effect. Figures of speech can contribute to *subtext*— meaning beyond the written words and their literal interpretation.

Some of the figures of speech used in fiction include:[12]

- *Elision*—dropped initial, middle, or final sound in a word. (They say nothin'. Rupert live 'bout five mile 'way.)
- *Ellipsis*—omission of words. (You bad!)
- *Euphemism*—substitution of a less offensive or more agreeable term for another. (Boyd stepped behind the bushes to *answer the call of nature*.)
- *Hyperbole*—exaggeration of a statement. (The harpoon weighed a *ton*.)
- *Idiom*—an expression whose meaning is not predictable from the usual meanings of its words. (After a two-year engagement, they *tied the knot* in front of family and friends.)

- *Innuendo*—a usage having a hidden, often sexual or derogatory, meaning in a sentence that makes sense whether it is detected or not. (At the end of their first date, Arty told Jenny he would like to see *more of her.*)
- *Irony*—the use of a word in a way that conveys a meaning opposite to its usual meaning. (Al saw that the thermometer had risen to three degrees Fahrenheit—a real *heat wave.*)
- *Parallelism*—use of similar structures in two or more clauses (Figures don't lie, but liars figure.)

A common technique for building an emotional connection with the reader is the use of comparative description employing the figures of speech *simile* or *metaphor.*

- *Metaphor*—stating that one entity *is* another for the purpose of suggesting a resemblance. (Number 64, the left tackle, was a *tank.*)
- *Simile*—comparing two things using *like* or *as.* (Number 64, the left tackle, was *as big and powerful as a tank.*)

Other figures of speech attribute humans, deities, animals, objects, concepts, or natural phenomena with the attributes of another. These include *anthropomorphism* (attributing human characteristics to something that isn't human), *prosopopoeia* (presenting a dead or absent person as being alive and present), and *zoomorphism* (presenting something as an animal that isn't an animal). Using *trans-* (for change) and *morph-* (for form), I call these techniques *transmorphic* description. For example, describing a human as a pit bull, a storm as evil, or a tree as stoic.

Avoid the following figures of speech unless they are intended for specific effect, such as humor.

- *Tautology*—needless repetition of a concept by using different words. Saying the same thing twice[13] (a round circle, frozen ice, liquid water, hot fire, retreating backward).
- *Circumlocution*—substituting or adding words to be ambiguous or to "talk around" a topic.[14] (Instead of saying *his great-grandfather*, saying *his father's father's father*.)

Metaphors can be very useful in description, but they can also be abused. A *mixed metaphor* combines unrelated elements and can result in incongruous comparisons. For example, *He's barking up the wrong tree* is a metaphor. And so is *He's up the creek without a paddle*. But *He's barking up the wrong creek* is a mixed metaphor.

Metaphors are not limited to a single word or phrase. If a metaphor continues into subsequent sentences or even throughout an entire story, it is referred to as an *extended metaphor*.[15] William Shakespeare wrote one of the most well-known extended metaphors in *As You Like It*.

"All the world's a stage. And all men and women merely players. They have their exits and their entrances. And one man in his time plays many parts." (*As You Like It*, Act II, Scene VII)[16]

Some figures of speech are so fresh and apt, people repeat them. Once a figure of speech gains widespread use, especially over a long span of time, it loses the freshness that initially made it so appealing; it becomes a kind of literary shorthand, a *cliché*. Writing filled with clichés appears lazy, trite, and hackneyed. As writers, we should strive for fresh language.

SPATIAL ORGANIZATION

Spatial organization refers to the order in which you describe the components of a setting or a complex object. Traditionally you begin with a wide viewpoint and then narrow to specifics, much as you would use a telescope to start with a panoramic view, and then focus in close for greater detail.

Beginning with a wide view is consistent with distant narration that approaches the story from afar and then narrows to specifics where appropriate. Here's an example of spatial organization that starts with a *distant* point of view.

> The starless sky showed no sign of light (panoramic). A gentle breeze whispered through leafless branches high overhead, and an owl hooted in the distance (treetop level). Flickering campfires sent shadows dancing across canvas tents nestled among stately trees (on the ground). Nearby, an armed guard slogged through rustling leaves and mud that sucked at his boots (a little closer). Freezing drizzle settled on Lemuel's cheeks as he peered into the darkness around him (up close and personal).

When writing from an *intimate* point of view, you may want to begin with up-close description and zoom out from there. For example,

> Freezing drizzle settled on Lemuel's cheeks as he peered into the darkness around him (up close and personal). Nearby, an armed guard slogged through rustling leaves and mud that sucked at his boots (nearby). Flickering camp-fires sent shadows dancing across canvas tents nestled among stately trees (ground level). A gentle breeze whis-

pered through leafless branches high overhead, and an owl hooted in the distance (treetop level). The starless sky showed no sign of light (panoramic).

The needs of the story should dictate which approach is more appropriate.

CLARITY

Have you ever had to read something twice to grasp its meaning? *Clarity* in writing is the quality of being instantly understandable or recognizable to the reader.[17] Put yourself in your reader's mind and imagine reading the passage for the first time. Do you have to pause and think about it? If you stumble over description, so will your reader. As in glassware, crystal clarity is the standard, a worthy goal for all of us.

QUANTITY

How much description is enough? How much is too much? In part, the amount of description depends upon the genre in which you're writing. Romances tend to be highly descriptive, often an expectation of readers for that genre. In science fiction and fantasy, the creation of an elaborate story world may require extensive description.

Regardless of the genre, with too little description the reader might not get the picture you intend to communicate. Too much description can bore the reader and stall the story. Too much description may deprive the reader of the satisfaction of "filling in the blanks" herself. An effective balance includes enough description to fuel the reader's imagination but not so much that it impedes the flow of the story. When in doubt, write just enough description to accomplish your objective.

OBTRUSIVENESS

Separate from the issue of quantity of description is the issue of obtrusiveness. *Obtrusiveness* is the degree to which description (regardless of amount) is noticeable, how much it stands out to the reader. How noticeable should description be?

The answer depends upon your objectives. If your intention is to write fast-paced, intimate, and immediate fiction, then you should strive for description that is so unobtrusive that the casual reader doesn't notice it. The goal of a writer striving for unobtrusive description is to have the reader get the benefit of description without noticing the words, to experience the story with minimal distraction.

A more stylistic writer might strive for elaborate description that, by its nature, draws attention to itself. Such obtrusive description puts distance between reader and story. Noticeable description may even knock the reader out of his suspended disbelief. Writing that is so flowery that it draws attention to itself is sometimes referred to as *purple prose*. Consider the following:

> Her silken, sun-kissed locks made a golden frame around her perfect, heart-shaped face. Soft, ruby-red lips curved up and crystalline sky-blue eyes sparkled as she looked down at the brilliant, beaming emerald clasped in her long, elegant, lily-white fingers.

Description may stand on its own, where the story narrator communicates the description directly to the reader. For example,

> All around were the forested hills of Yellowstone National Park. In the distance a ghostlike column of steam rose above the trees, a reminder that Native Americans once viewed the Yellowstone area as a home of evil spirits, a portal to the underworld.

Stand-alone description draws attention to itself; it's obtrusive. If your goal is to write intimate, immediate fiction, avoid the use of obtrusive description.

Description may also be mixed with other fiction-writing modes such as action, dialogue, introspection, recollection, or sensation, in effect becoming *disguised description*. For example, you can have description appear to flow through the mind of a viewpoint character, as introspection. To accomplish this, just place a sentence with the viewpoint character as the subject in front of the description.

> Park Ranger Travis O'Brian braced himself as he held a climbing line snug against his backside. All around him were the forested hills of Yellowstone National Park and the scent of pine. In the distance a ghostlike column of steam rose above the trees, reminding him that Native Americans once viewed the Yellowstone area as a home of evil spirits, a portal to the underworld.

How you handle description can affect how much the reader notices it. The more a reader notices description, the less he can suspend his own disbelief. And willing suspension of disbelief makes a great deal of difference in how much the reader enjoys the story.

TAKEAWAYS

1. *Vividness* is the degree to which description brings a story to life.
2. Word choice is the foundation of description.
3. Details add depth and credibility to description.
4. Details range from irrelevant to telling.
5. Concrete nouns create more vivid description than do abstract nouns.
6. Specific nouns portray more robust description than do general nouns.
7. Singular nouns create different images than do plural nouns.
8. The connotation of a word may be quite different that its denotation.
9. Conciseness requires the elimination of unnecessary words.
10. Eliminate intensifiers and qualifiers from your description.
11. Avoid expletives in description.
12. Use syntax to control the effectiveness of description.
13. Various figures of speech may be useful additions to description, while others should be avoided.
14. *Spatial organization* refers to the order in which a setting or complex object is described.
15. *Clarity* in writing is the quality of being instantly understandable or recognizable.
16. Consistent with the genre, limit the quantity of description to only that which is needed.
17. *Obtrusiveness* in description is the degree to which it is noticeable to the reader.

In the next chapter we'll explore how information may be shared through exposition.

EXPOSITION

The fiction-writing mode that conveys information.

CHAPTER CONTENTS
Delivery methods
Quantity
Selection
Timing
Scenes and sequels

In fiction writing, *exposition* is the mode for conveying information—facts, explanation, or opinion. The fiction-writing-mode exposition has a tarnished reputation, and for good reason. In their book *Good Advice on Writing,* William and Leonard Safire quote Voltaire:

Woe to the author determined to teach!
The best way to be boring is to leave nothing out.[1]

Exposition, if handled obtrusively, can kill plot momentum and stall a story. It can be tedious and uninteresting. A classic example of obtrusive exposition is in *Moby-Dick*, where Herman Melville breaks away from his otherwise fascinating story for entire chapters to tell about the folklore, anatomy, and habits of whales.

If exposition carries such a burden, why do fiction writers use it at all? Because exposition can provide the perspective, dimension, and context that help a story make sense and give it depth. For example,

> Around the table were three of the most senior officers governing Upper Canada. With York as its capital, the province included vast territory stretching west along the Great Lakes and beyond.

Here, exposition puts the men around the table in perspective, adds geographic and political depth, and provides context to characters, plot, and setting.

Exposition can also be an effective means of creating drama.

> If the new nation didn't pay more attention to the concerns of the northeastern states, New England might break away, form a new nation, and realign with Great Britain.

In the example above, exposition provides information that raises the stakes: a threat to the future of the nation. Exposition can turn the entertaining act of reading fiction into a thought-provoking, educational experience.

The concept of writing exposition may appear to be simple, but *how* you reveal information is as important as *what* information you reveal. Exposition may be delivered through three methods: narrative exposition, characters, or expository devices.

NARRATIVE EXPOSITION

The simplest way to present information is for the all-knowing, impersonal, and invisible narrator to state it. In *narrative exposition*, the narrator of the story presents information directly to the reader without any pretext of channeling it through a character or exposing it through some sort of prop.

Narrative exposition has the advantage of simplicity, but the price is *authorial intrusion*, the author revealing himself to the reader. No matter how deeply a reader submerges herself into a story, she knows subconsciously that an author put the words on paper. But if the author intrudes too much into the story, the reader may be jolted out of her suspended disbelief. Here's an example of narrative exposition.

Slade carried a switchblade in his coat pocket.

Narrative exposition is undisguised communication of information directly from the narrator to the reader and is thus obtrusive.

THROUGH CHARACTERS

Characters may provide information through what they say, hear, see, smell, feel, think, or recall. Here's an example of exposition through dialogue.

Becky grabbed Hanrahan's arm. "Be careful, sweetie. I heard that Slade carries a switchblade in his pocket."

Here's an example of exposition through recollection.

> Hanrahan paused before stepping into the barroom. He recalled hearing something about how Slade had killed a snitch in Chinatown. With a switchblade.

Here's the same information being revealed through a character's thoughts.

> Hanrahan paused before stepping into the barroom. What if Slade carried a hidden weapon? Like a switchblade.

Providing information that flows through a character allows the reader to continue his suspended disbelief, but there are pitfalls. A potential problem is when your character presents information that is too obviously for the reader's education. Readers can tell if characters are being used as a device for presenting information, in effect using them as puppets to spout information. Even worse is when a single character pontificates, in the fiction writer's version of a soliloquy. For example,

> "As you know, Becky," said Hanrahan, "Slade carries a switchblade in his coat pocket."

EXPOSITORY DEVICES

Various devices may be used to convey information. Classic examples include such props as treasure maps and messages in bottles. Others include newspaper clippings, letters, diaries, and trial transcriptions. The advancement of technology has provided new expository devices: emails, text messages, podcasts, and surveillance-camera tapes. In the world of science fiction and fantasy, expository devices are limited only by the writer's imagination (think *Star Trek* and *Harry Potter*).

Here's an example of using an expository device.

> As Hanrahan approached the bar, a kid approached him. "Hey, mister, a lady across the street asked me to bring you this note."
> Hanrahan unfolded the paper and read, *Be careful. Slade carries a switchblade.*

OTHER ISSUES

Other issues related to effective exposition include quantity, selection of information, timing, and exposition in scenes and sequels.

QUANTITY

How much information is appropriate? Too little, and the reader won't fully understand the story, or the story may lack depth. Too much at one time may become an *information dump,* which stalls the story. In general, exposition should be no longer than necessary to do its job.

The amount of information presented in a story may vary, from incidental to entire chapters built around information. Think of the importance of information in novels such as Dan Brown's *Da Vinci Code* and Michael Crichton's *Jurassic Park.* Even entire genres, such as sci-fi, crime fiction, and historical fiction, may be filled with exposition, sometimes intricately detailed information.

Fiction packed with exposition can be mind-numbingly boring, or it can be fascinating, depending upon how you convey that information. The more exposition presented in a story, the more that information needs to be intrinsically interesting. Even riveting information in substantial quantities requires skillful presentation to avoid turning off the reader.

SELECTION OF INFORMATION

Which information should you include and which should you exclude? The reader doesn't need to know everything, just the important stuff. With this in mind, each bit of exposition needs justification for its inclusion in the story. To qualify for selection, information needs to advance the story, either through characterization, plot development, setting improvement, or theme enhancement.

TIMING

When is the right time to introduce new information? You want to present information when the reader needs it—not before he needs it and not after he needs it. Wait until the information is relevant to the storyline.[2] Readers are interested in explanation only *after* you have aroused their curiosity about something that needs explaining.[3]

EXPOSITION IN SCENES AND SEQUELS

In fiction, a *scene* is a passage of writing in which a character attempts to achieve a goal. A scene is largely about action, so little exposition is usually involved. When you present information in a scene, weave that information into the action so you don't interrupt the story.

In fiction, a *sequel* is the reflective aftermath that follows a scene. Whether or not the character's attempt to achieve his objective was successful, his reaction is likely to be emotional. As in real life, emotion is often followed by a period of thinking.[4] The proximity of emotion and thinking makes sequels fertile ground for presenting information.

Ansen Dibell, in *Plot*, appreciates the linkage of information and emotion: "We tend to remember best the information that comes to us surrounded by highly charged emotion."[5] Think of where you were on September 11, 2001. Can you recall portions of that day in detail? Just as you can recall specific events from 9/11, your readers can best absorb and remember information when you present it in highly emotional situations. For example,

Rachel's mind reeled. Just that morning she had read that Robert Fulton had died. She remembered meeting the famous inventor and steamship operator at the Madisons' dinner party several years before. Inspired by Fulton's success in running steamboats on the Hudson and Mississippi rivers, enterprising businessmen were launching steamboats as fast as they could build them. There was renewed talk of building the canal Fulton had championed— from Albany to Lake Erie.

TAKEAWAYS

1. Exposition can add perspective, dimension, and context to a story.
2. Exposition may be delivered through three means: narrative exposition, characters, and expository devices.
3. Narrative exposition presents information directly from the narrator to the reader.
4. Characters may provide information through what they say, hear, see, smell, feel, think, or recall.
5. Avoid making characters obvious puppets for spouting information.

6. Expository devices vary by genre but can be an effective means of delivering information.

7. Too little information and the reader may not fully understand the story or the story may lack depth.

8. Too much information risks stalling the story.

9. The reader doesn't need to know everything, only what enhances plot, characterization, setting, or theme.

10. Present information only when the reader needs it—not before and not after.

11. Readers are interested in information only after you have aroused their curiosity.

12. In scenes, weave information into the action.

13. Use the emotion and thinking of sequels to effectively present information.

In the next chapter we'll transport readers across time, distance, and viewpoint though transition.

18

TRANSITION

The fiction-writing mode that moves from one place, time, or character to another.

CHAPTER CONTENTS
Transitions and the elements of fiction
Structural units of fiction writing
Transitions in time
Point-of-view changes
Transitions in and out of flashbacks
Types of transition
Transitional words and phrases
Fiction-writing modes as transitions
Punctuation as transition
Paragraph, section, and chapter breaks as transition
Location of transitions
Timing of transitions
Length of transitions
Selection of transitions
Consistency vs. variety in transitions

Headings and datelines as transitions
Transitional devices
Obtrusiveness of transitions

Transitions are the words and punctuation that facilitate the flow of stories by leading the reader from one character to another, from one place to another, or from one time to another.

What can the television series *Star Trek* teach us about transition? *Star Trek* routinely shows characters transporting through space ("Beam me up, Scotty!"). Some episodes shift people back and forth though time via wormholes and other gaps in the space-time continuum. In the world of fiction writing, these leaps through time and space are called *transitions*.

The ability of *Star Trek* characters to teleport from one location to another and move backward and forward in time adds depth and complexity. Fiction, by its very nature, involves movement of one sort or another, and that requires transition. Even though fiction is filled with transitions, they can be so subtle and effective that a reader may not notice that a transition has occurred.

Jessica Page Morrell states, "Crafting transitions might not make you feel like a creative genius, and it doesn't qualify as one of the captivating parts of storytelling, but it reveals your respect for your reader." She also cautions: "Transitions are your way of showing courtesy to the reader, but do not imagine your reader is an intellectual invalid."[1]

Effective transitions balance the need to be helpful to the reader while trusting the reader to "get it," and to "fill in the blanks" where necessary.

TRANSITIONS AND THE ELEMENTS OF FICTION

Transitions play a role in each of the fundamental elements of fiction (plot, character, setting, theme, and style). Transitions pave the way for readers as the story moves through location and time; i.e., settings. Transitions help the reader shift from one viewpoint character to another in multiple-viewpoint stories. Transitions link the structural units of plot from the smallest to the largest (between stimulus and response; scenes and sequels; and beginnings, middles, and endings).

STRUCTURAL UNITS OF FICTION WRITING

Distinct from the structural units of plot are the structural units of fiction writing. The smallest units of writing are words, phrases, clauses, sentences, and paragraphs. Two or more paragraphs with common purpose may be referred to as a *passage* or a *segment* of writing.

A segment of writing in which a character attempts to achieve a goal is a *scene*. A passage of writing in which a character reflects on the outcome of a scene is called a *sequel*. Sometimes a segment of writing is neither a scene nor a sequel: for example, a passage of summary, exposition, or description.

A *chapter* is a segment of writing delineated by a chapter beginning and a chapter ending. A chapter may include one or more scenes and/or one or more sequels. A chapter may also include segments of writing that are neither scenes nor sequels. A chapter may include two or more *sections*, passages separated by section breaks. Some novels, especially long ones, may be further divided into *books* or *parts*, each including one or more chapters.

Each of these units has a role. As a writer you need to recognize each, know its role, and know how to use it to construct your story. For example, a new scene may begin at the end of a chapter, and then continue in the next chapter—or even later in the book. Consider a chapter in which a hiker stumbles off a trail and finds herself clutching a rocky ledge atop a precipice. Such an event would certainly create a new short-term goal for the character (avoiding a fall), which would mark the beginning of a new scene. When placed at the end of a chapter, such a scene fragment is referred to as a *cliffhanger*.

TRANSITIONS IN TIME

By far the most common transitions in fiction are those reflecting changes in time. In fiction, time must always be accounted for.[2] Whether hours, days, or years have elapsed between segments, the author needs to communicate this, and transitions can do that. Transitions allow the author to skip the dull and the mundane, condensing time and space so the characters can get to the interesting stuff.

POINT-OF-VIEW CHANGES

Some stories, because of their scope, interconnection, and depth, need to be told through the viewpoint of more than one character. When more than one viewpoint is used, the reader has access to a wider range of insight.

The use of more than one viewpoint character, however, entails risks and challenges. The reader may become confused as to from which viewpoint the story is being told. Bouncing in and out of the mind of more than one character can disorient the reader. To avoid this, follow these rules about transitions from one point-of-view character to another:

- Use only one viewpoint character for each writing segment.
- In each writing segment, establish the viewpoint character immediately.
- When changing viewpoint character, provide clear signals to the reader, such as a chapter break or a section break.

TRANSITIONS IN AND OUT OF FLASHBACKS

A *flashback* is a scene that interrupts the main timeline of the story while the character relives a past event. You can transition in and out of a flashback as follows:

- Anchor your character in the story's present with a sensory perception, some incidental action, or something that reminds the character of the past event.
- Assuming most of your story is written in simple past tense (He *stopped* by his friend's house), write a sentence or two in which you change the verb tense to past perfect (He *had stopped* by his friend's house once before, fifteen years ago).
- Once this transition is completed, switch back to simple past tense and let the character experience the scene (the flashback).
- Transition back to the main timeline of the story by writing a sentence or two in past perfect tense.
- Return the character to the story's present by reintroducing the sensory perception or incidental action used prior to the flashback.

For example,

> Roxy pulled a plate from the steaming dishwater and rinsed
> it. She had been doing dishes when the sheriff's car had
> pulled into the driveway. (Write the flashback scene in
> simple past tense, as if it were happening in the "now" of the
> story.) Roxy dried the plate and set it in the rack to the side.
> She reached for another dish and realized the water had
> cooled.

TYPES OF TRANSITION

Transitions may be created in three ways: transitional words or
phrases, fiction-writing modes, or punctuation.

TRANSITIONAL WORDS AND PHRASES

Simple transitions may be in the form of subordinate clauses
placed at the beginning of a sentence or paragraph. For example,

> Two hours later, Bob...
> Meanwhile, back at the ranch,...
> The next morning on the other side of the world...

They take the reader quickly and smoothly from one time or place
to another, adding coherence to the story.

FICTION-WRITING MODES AS TRANSITIONS

Transitions themselves may be considered a fiction-writing mode.
But transitions can also be delivered through each of the other ten
fiction-writing modes, thus providing the writer a wide selection
from which to choose the best means for dealing with a specific

challenge. Here are examples to signal that the story has moved forward three hours:

- NARRATION: We jump ahead three hours where we find Rowdy...
- SUMMARIZATION: Three hours later, Rowdy...
- DESCRIPTION: The scorching sun blazed across the afternoon sky for another three hours, and Rowdy...
- ACTION: Rowdy reined his horse to a stop. After three hours of hard riding, they both needed a rest.
- CONVERSATION: "It's three o'clock," said Rowdy. "Gus swore he would be here at noon."
- EXPOSITION: Rowdy had been sitting in the saloon for three hours, expecting Gus to show up as promised.
- SENSATION: A blast of wind chilled Rowdy. The temperature had dropped at least twenty degrees during the last three hours.
- INTROSPECTION: Rowdy glanced at the clock over the bar and realized Gus was three hours late.
- EMOTION: Rowdy slammed the shot glass on the bar. Three hours was the longest he'd ever waited for anyone.
- RECOLLECTION: The clock over the saloon bar chimed three o'clock. Rowdy looked up from his cards and recalled that just that morning Gus had promised to meet him here at noon.

PUNCTUATION AS TRANSITION

Punctuation is a system of signals that shows how writing should be read. Each item of punctuation indicates change of some sort. In other words, each facilitates transition.

Transition exists on three levels of punctuation, which I call microlevel, mesolevel, and macrolevel.

- *Microlevel* punctuates sentences: periods, commas, semicolons, colons, dashes, ellipses, question marks, and exclamation points.
- *Mesolevel* defines paragraphs with paragraph breaks.
- *Macrolevel* delineates sections and chapters with the bullhorns of punctuation: section breaks and chapter breaks.

PARAGRAPH, SECTION, AND CHAPTER BREAKS AS TRANSITION

You may be surprised to learn that paragraph breaks, section breaks, and chapter breaks are punctuation, but they are.[3] *Paragraph breaks* mark the transition between paragraphs. Section breaks signal a change of viewpoint character or other transition within a chapter, and in a manuscript they are indicated with a blank line.

Readers expect the end of one chapter and the beginning of another to coincide with changes of one sort or another: time, location, or viewpoint character. If the changes signaled by a chapter break are slight (little or no change in time or location), then punctuation alone, in the form of a chapter break, might serve as adequate transition.

Punctuation is an effective shorthand for creating transition, and it should not be overlooked as an opportunity to enhance the seamless flow of a story.

Words, phrases, punctuation, and fiction-writing modes might be the means of delivering transitions, but that still leaves many other issues to consider: location, timing, length, selection, consistency vs. variety, headings and datelines, transitional devices, and obtrusiveness.

LOCATION OF TRANSITIONS

Transitions may appear anywhere there is a change within the story, and story structure dictates the location of changes. Story structure, especially regarding plot, exists on several levels. On a microlevel, plot consists of stimulus and response (sometimes referred to as "action and reaction"). On a macrolevel, plot has a beginning, a middle, and an ending. Plot also has a midlevel structure of segments called *scenes* and *sequels*. Fiction often has another level of structure that includes chapters and sections.

These structural units don't just butt against each other—they often require some transition to mark the change from one to another. So story structure looks like this:

Stimulus transition response
Scene transition sequel
Chapter/section transition chapter/section
Beginning transition middle transition ending

Although changes requiring a transition may happen anywhere within a structural unit, the most significant changes occur *between* structural units of a story.

TIMING OF TRANSITIONS

Writers have three distinct timeframes to alert the reader to a change: before, during, and after.

A change may be signaled *before* it occurs. For example, *Clyde grabbed Gramps by the shoulder. "I'll meet you back at the ranch in three hours."* Here, dialogue marks an upcoming change in time (three hours) and a new location (the ranch).

Transition *during* the change may be portrayed by various means, including action, summary, and dialogue. For example, *Clyde took the shortcut and arrived at the ranch three hours later.* Here, a change in time (three hours later) and a new location (the ranch) are summarized as they occur through narration.

A chapter break marks a change while it is occurring. For example, Chapter 3 might be told from the viewpoint of Miss Agnes in the saloon, but Chapter 4 might be told from the viewpoint of Gramps at his ranch.

Another shorthand means of communicating a change while it is occurring is with a section break. For example, the first section of a chapter may be from the viewpoint of Ishmael on the *Pequod's* deck, and after a blank line to signal a section break, the viewpoint shifts to Ahab in his cabin. By default, a section break coincides with the change: at the end of the previous section, the change has *not yet occurred*, but it has *already occurred* before the beginning of the next section.

Further transitional opportunities are available *after* the change. For example, *At the ranch, Clyde eased out of the saddle. He had been riding for three hours.* Here, a change in time (three hours) and new location (the ranch) are signaled with a combination of action and narration.

Depending on the circumstances, you may communicate a change using all three timeframes. For example,

Clyde grabbed Gramps by the shoulder. "I'll meet you back at the ranch in three hours." (Transition signaled *before* the change)

The beginning of a page with a new chapter heading signals a chapter break. (Transition delineated *during* the change)

As Clyde eased out of the saddle, Gramps hobbled out of the bunkhouse door with a sawed-off shotgun. "You're late!" (Transition marked *after* the change)

LENGTH OF TRANSITIONS

Transitions may range from being very short (one word or a single punctuation mark) to lengthy (paragraphs or pages). Inadequate transitions risk jarring the reader out of her suspended disbelief if she must reread the passage to find the transition and reorient herself. Long transitions risk impeding the pace of the story.

In *The Marshall Plan for Novel Writing*, Evan Marshall likens transitions and the various units of a story to a pearl necklace. "The best-made strands...have tiny knots in the string between the pearls, to hold them tightly in place and keep the necklace strong."[4]

David Madden, in the *Writer's Digest Handbook of Novel Writing*, seems to agree: "Keep transitions crisp. Do it quickly, instead of sending readers trudging over a long, elaborately constructed transition bridge."[5]

SELECTION OF TRANSITIONS

Much of writing has to do with making choices, and transitions are no exception: an author must decide which transitions to employ. Readers don't need to follow characters through every twist and turn, especially when performing activities familiar to the reader. A good rule of thumb is that if you can omit a transition without confusing the reader, do so.

CONSISTENCY VS. VARIETY IN TRANSITIONS

Fiction writing often involves a struggle to find an appropriate balance between extremes. In transitions, the balance is between establishing helpful patterns and avoiding repetition.

Jessica Page Morrell in *Between the Lines* recognizes the benefit of patterns: "When you use a pattern that the reader can easily recognize, the pattern, in a sense, serves as a transition."[6] For example, in multiple-point-of-view fiction, repeated use of section breaks to signal a change of viewpoint character will accustom the reader to the changes. Likewise, limiting each chapter to one viewpoint character is, in effect, using chapter breaks to signal a change of viewpoint character.

At the other end of the spectrum, Morrell advises writers to "Be sure not to overuse a particular transitional approach. For instance, many writers always use setting details and weather to announce a change of location or scene.... When overused they become dull.[7] Transitions need to be varied," continues Morrell, "sometimes unobtrusive, sometimes colorful, and always graceful. Expand your transition repertoire and find fresh ways to indicate the passing of time and influence the mood of your story."[8]

HEADINGS AND DATELINES AS TRANSITIONS

Two obtrusive forms of direct narration closely related to chapter breaks and section breaks are headings and datelines. For example,

Chapter 1: Jack
Chapter 2: Jill

Tom Clancy used datelines extensively in *Red Storm Rising*, a novel depicting multiple viewpoint characters scattered geographically. Examples include chapter and section headings such as:

USS NIMITZ
HILL 152, ICELAND
KIEV, THE UKRAINE
DOVER AIR FORCE BASE, DELAWARE

Transitions in headlines may also include dates and time:

MAY 1812
DAY THREE
24:00

TRANSITIONAL DEVICES

Various devices may portray change:

- Lighting, shadow, sun, stars, and moon (Jack and Jill held each other as the full moon worked its way across the sky.)
- Weather (The storm raged for twenty minutes, then disappeared as quickly as it developed.)
- Seasons, years, eras (Andrew watched fall become winter, and winter turn to spring.)
- Objects (The sail on the horizon grew closer as the morning passed.)
- Mundane activities (Bodie washed the dishes, then took a nap.)

- Character's appearance, health (Mike's hair turned from brown to salt-and-pepper gray, and then to white as...)
- Time, date (Sunday, at noon, Ahab called the crew together.)
- Activities, interruptions (As Sarah was about to reveal the big news, her phone rang, cutting through the moment and forcing her to step outside. The conversation hung in the air, unresolved, as the group shifted uncomfortably in their seats.)[9]

OBTRUSIVENESS OF TRANSITIONS

Transitions should lead the reader through the story seamlessly. Obtrusive transitions may jolt the reader out of the fictive dream.

Big changes, such as a large shifts in time, location, or viewpoint, may require pronounced transitions, such as section or chapter breaks accompanied by appropriate transitional content.

The challenge is to create transitions that are effective yet unobtrusive. Regarding transitions, the ultimate compliment a reader could pay to an author is asking, "What transitions?"

TAKEAWAYS

1. Transitions link the structural units of plot.
2. Transitions help account for time in fiction.
3. Transitions smooth the change between point-of-view characters.
4. Transitions can guide the reader in and out of flashbacks.
5. Transitions may be as simple as a few words or phrases.
6. Transition may be accomplished through any of the fiction-writing modes.

7. Punctuation facilitates transition at three levels, which I call microlevel, mesolevel, and macrolevel.

8. Paragraph, section, and chapter breaks signal transition.

9. Transitions may happen anywhere in a story, but the most significant changes occur between structural units of a story.

10. Transition may be signaled in three timeframes in relation to a change: before, during, and after.

11. Transitions may range in length from very short to paragraphs or even pages.

12. If a transition can be eliminated without confusing the reader, do so.

13. Patterns of writing and format may provide useful transition.

14. Variety in transitions may help avoid distracting repetition.

15. Headlines and dates may assist in transitions.

16. Change may be portrayed through various transitional devices.

17. Strive for effective, yet unobtrusive, transitions.

This concludes the last chapter about a specific fiction-writing mode. In the next chapter, I'll (1) demonstrate how to expand the eleven fiction-writing modes into dozens more, (2) identify which modes are the most intimate and immediate, (3) reveal what "Show. Don't tell." really means, and (4) explain how to put fiction-writing modes to work immediately through troubleshooting.

PART V

OVER THE RAINBOW

NEW PERSPECTIVES

CHAPTER CONTENTS
Expanding the universe of modes
Which modes are the most intimate and immediate
The real meaning of "Show. Don't tell."
Troubleshooting with fiction-writing modes

THE SPECTRUM OF FICTION-WRITING MODES

Painters have only three primary colors with which to work (red, yellow, and blue), yet from these three blossom a seemingly limitless spectrum with which artists create masterpieces. Fiction writers have *eleven* fiction-writing modes with which to create masterpieces. Just as painters may combine primary colors in different proportions to create a vast array of colors and shades, writers may combine fiction-writing modes to meet the needs of a story.

We've explored eleven fiction-writing modes one at a time. What if each mode could be joined with the others? After eliminating the duplicate combinations, that means fifty-five new modes. Added to the original eleven modes, that means a total of sixty-six permutations!

You're probably already familiar with some ways fiction-writing modes can be combined. How about *narrative description? Narrative summary? Narrative exposition? Expository dialogue?*

You may already be combining fiction-writing modes but don't realize it. Combining dialogue with transition creates *transitional dialogue* ("We sailed all night, but no land was visible in the morning."). Combining dialogue with description creates *descriptive dialogue* ("That little black dress shows off your figure, and it highlights the color of your hair."). Combining dialogue with sensation creates *sensory dialogue* ("New cologne? I detect a hint of leather. And a touch of bourbon.").

I'm not suggesting that all fifty-five combinations will be useful in each of your writing projects. The expanded universe of modes, however, provides you with additional flexibility to meet the specific needs of the task at hand, to engage the reader, and to bring that writing to life.

INTIMACY AND IMMEDIACY

With so many potential combinations, which modes should you use to write any particular passage of fiction? As a writer, only you can decide that, but be aware that not all fiction-writing modes are created equal.

Some of them are more intimate and immediate than others. The most distant and delayed (the least intimate and immediate) are the ones in which the narrator talks directly to the reader; i.e., description, exposition, narration, transition, and summarization. If your goal is to write with intimacy and immediacy, you want to minimize the use of those modes.

The most intimate and immediate fiction-writing modes are those in which the character may experience the story as it is happening: action, conversation, introspection, emotion, sensation, and recollection. If your goal is to write with intimacy and immediacy—and it should be—then you'll certainly want to emphasize these modes.

SHOW. DON'T TELL.

What constitutes showing, and what constitutes telling? Writing that *shows* tends to be written in fiction-writing modes with intimacy and immediacy; i.e., action, conversation, emotion, sensation, introspection, and recollection (the story being *shown* through the mind of the character). Writing that *tells* tends to be written in fiction-writing modes with distance and delay; i.e., narration, exposition, description, transition, and summarization (the story being *told* by the narrator).

If your intention is to show rather than tell, emphasize fiction-writing modes with intimacy and immediacy and deemphasize modes with distance and delay.

TROUBLESHOOTING WITH FICTION-WRITING MODES

Troubleshooting is one way you can put your new understanding of fiction-writing modes to use. Select a passage of writing you would like to improve. Read each sentence carefully. Note in the margin which fiction-writing mode (or combination of modes) you used to create it.

Assuming your goal is to write with intimacy and immediacy, your troubleshooting path becomes clear. Revisit each sentence in your passage and consider recasting the sentence using one or more of the intimate and immediate fiction-writing modes. For specifics and examples, revisit the chapters for each fiction-writing mode.

I hope you have enjoyed this exploration of fiction-writing modes. We've studied the *concept* of these modes, examined all eleven modes in detail, and seen how they can be combined to create fifty-five new modes. We've reviewed the subjects of distance and immediacy, and seen how the choice of modes affects "Show. Don't tell," and learned how to troubleshoot with fiction-writing modes. I hope this new information helps you fulfill your story-telling dreams.

SHARE THE WISDOM!

I think you'll notice a real difference in your approach to writing now you know more about the eleven modes of fiction writing, and I'm excited about what you're going to create. Take a moment now to share this information with more writers.

Simply by sharing your honest opinion of this book and a little about how it's informed your work, you'll show new readers where they can find this book and give them the inspiration they need to explore these eleven modes.

LEAVE A REVIEW!

Thank you so much for your support. I wish you every success in your writing career.

Scan the QR code below

EXPLORE OTHER WORKS BY MIKE KLAASSEN

NONFICTION

How to Write a Novel That Matters: Crafting Stories with the Power to Captivate, Enlighten, and Inspire

Scenes and Sequels: How to Write Page-Turning Fiction

Third-Person Possessed: How to Write Page-Turning Fiction for 21st Century Readers

HISTORICAL FICTION

Backlash: A War of 1812 Novel

YOUNG-ADULT NOVELS

Cracks

The Brute

KLAASSEN'S CLASSIC FOLKTALES

Jack and the Beanstalk: The Old English Story Told as a Novella

Cinderella: The Brothers Grimm Story Told as a Novella

The Frog Prince: The Brothers Grimm Story Told as a Novella

Hansel and Gretel: The Brothers Grimm Story Told as a Novella

SUPERPOWER LIFE SKILLS

Superpower Life Skill for Teens with Ambition: How to Master Resilience, Conflict Resolution, Teamwork, Money Management, Critical Thinking, and More to Become Your Best Self

ABOUT THE AUTHOR

Mike Klaassen writes action-filled stories about young protagonists confronting significant challenges. His novels include *The Brute, Cracks*, and *Backlash: A War of 1812 Novel*.

Driven by a passion for continuous learning, Mike delved into the art of storytelling, producing a series of books about the craft of writing fiction. These books offer practical guidance for aspiring writers and illuminate the processes behind compelling story-telling.

Fusing his love for folklore and his interest in writing fiction, Mike initiated "Klaassen's Classic Folktales," a collection that retells ancient stories as novellas. Through this series, he breathes new life into time-honored tales, offering readers of all ages a fresh perspective on these enduring stories.

In 2024, Mike wrote *Superpower Life Skills for Teens with Ambition: How to Master Resilience, Conflict Resolution, Teamwork, Money Management, Critical Thinking, and More to Become Your Best Self.*

INDEX

abstract noun, 213

accent, 126, 183

active voice, 98

adverb, 100, 155, 156

aftermath, 31, 113, 239

anthropomorphism, 222

attribution, 68

attribution clause, 153

authorial intrusion, 234

backstory, 83

brevity, 119

cause and effect, 64, 109

chapter break, 251

character change, 63

chronological order, 104

circumlocution, 223

clarity, 226

cliché, 49, 224

climax, 57, 119

colloquialism, 126, 179

colon, 182, 194, 250

concrete noun, 213

conflict, 136, 137

connotation, 215

context, 46, 216

contractions, 180

dash, 195, 250

dateline, 256

denotation, 215

dependent clause, 107

detail, 102, 117, 212

dialect, 126, 183

dialogue attribution, 161

direct address, 146

direct dialogue, 139
direct introspection, 73
direct-address narration, 203
disguised description, 229
disguised narration, 205
distance, 48
distant point of view, 225
elision, 183, 221
ellipsis, 195, 221
em dash, 195
emotional experience, 211
epiphany, 78
euphemism, 221
exclamation point, 192
expletive, 217
expletive attributive, 218
expository device, 83, 237
extended metaphor, 223
extrasensory perception, 37
figure of speech, 220
filter verb, 206, 208
flashback, 87
flow of dialogue, 162
font change, 198
forecasting narration, 203
fragment, 182
frustration, 51
future story, 83
future tense, 95
general noun, 214
goal, 137
grammar, 126, 182
grammatical tense, 95
heading, 256
hyperbole, 221
idiom, 221
immediacy, 74, 75, 94, 95, 101, 217
immediate, 99, 101
incidental action, 107, 111, 170, 191, 193
indirect introspection, 73, 74

inflection, 126, 171

information dump, 237

innuendo, 221

intensifier, 216

intensity, 31, 53

internalization, 64

intimacy, 71, 74, 75, 77

intimate point of view, 225

intuition, 11, 37

irony, 221

italics, 67, 198

melodrama, 46, 47, 54, 55, 192

metaphor, 222

milieu, 50

misdirected dialogue, 139

mixed metaphor, 223

monologue, 123

motivation, 63

narrative distance, 71

narrative exposition, 234

narrator, 48

noun, 165

number, 196

oblique dialogue, 139

obtrusive narration, 203

obtrusiveness, 258

on-the-nose dialogue, 139

paragraph, 69, 189

paragraph break, 251

parallel dialogue, 138

parallelism, 222

passive voice, 98

past-perfect tense, 96

period, 187

physically impossible, 107, 155

plural noun, 215

present tense, 95

profanity, 176, 218

prosopopoeia, 222

punctuation, 182, 250

purple prose, 228

qualifier, 217

question mark, 194, 251

quotation mark, 67, 187, 194

real time, 99

redundant modifier, 216

reminder narration, 203

repetition, 47, 154

resistance, 109, 137, 138

sacrifice, 56

said, 153

scene, 64, 111, 113

scene climax, 58

section break, 251

semicolon, 182, 194, 250

sentence structure, 126

sentimental, 54

sequel, 64, 113

Show. Don't tell., 115

silence, 142

simile, 222

simple past tense, 95

simultaneous, 105, 107

singular noun, 215

sixth sense, 37

slang, 179

spatial organization, 224

specific noun, 214

stakes, 137

stimulus and response, 64, 109

story tense, 95

strong verb, 97

subtext, 221

subtext dialogue, 141

symbol, 31

syntactic expletive, 217

syntax, 220

tautology, 223

telling detail, 102, 213

theme, 13, 66

time, 32, 116, 224
to be, 97
transmorphic description, 222
unnecessary word, 216
unobtrusive description, 227
unobtrusive narration, 204
verb of attribution, 153
verb of recollection, 85
verb of sensation, 24
verb of thought, 70
verisimilitude, 23
vividness, 211
voice, 13, 145
weak verb, 98, 101
word choice, 126, 211
zoomorphism, 222

BIBLIOGRAPHY

Aristotle. *Poetics*. Penguin Classics. 1996. ISBN: 9780140446364.

Baldwin, Faith (1893-1978). "From *The Writer* Archive: Infuse characters with sincere emotion" (first published in April 1962). *The Writer*, March 2008, 20-21.

Bell, James Scott. "Fiction: Creating active dialogue." *Writer's Digest*, June 2003, 16-21.

Bell, James Scott. *Plot & Structure: Techniques and Exercises for Crafting a Plot That Grips Readers from Start to Finish*. Write Great Fiction series. Cincinnati: Writer's Digest Books, 2004. ISBN: 9781582972947.

Bell, Susan. *The Artful Edit: On the Practice of Editing Yourself*. New York: W. W. Norton & Company, 2007. ISBN: 9780393057522.

Bickham, Jack M. *Scene & Structure: How to Construct Fiction with Scene-by-Scene Flow, Logic and Readability*. The Elements of Fiction Writing series. Cincinnati: Writer's Digest Books, 1993. ISBN: 9780898795516.

Bickham, Jack M. *The 38 Most Common Fiction Writing Mistakes (and How to Avoid Them)*. Cincinnati: Writer's Digest Books, 1992. ISBN: 9780898798210.

Browne, Renni and David King. *Self-Editing for Fiction Writers: How to Edit Yourself into Print*. 2nd edition. New York: Harper Resource, an imprint of HarperCollins Publishers, Inc., 2004. ISBN: 9780060545697.

Cappon, Rene J. *Associated Press Guide to Punctuation*. New York: Basic Books, a member of the Perseus Books Group, 2003. ISBN: 9780738207858.

Card, Orson Scott. *Characters & Viewpoint*. The Elements of Fiction Writing series. Cincinnati: Writer's Digest Books, 1988. ISBN: 9780898793079.

Chiarella, Tom. *Writing Dialogue: How to Create Memorable Voices and Fictional Conversations that Crackle with Wit, Tension and Nuance*. Cincinnati: Story Press, an imprint of F & W Publications, Inc., 1998. ISBN: 9781884910326.

The Chicago Manual of Style. 17th ed. Chicago: University of Chicago Press, 2017. ISBN: 9780226287058.

Dibell, Ansen. *Plot: How to Build Short Stories and Novels that Don't Sag, Fizzle, or Trail Off in Scraps of Frustrated Revision—and How to Rescue Stories that Do*. The Elements of Fiction Writing series. Cincinnati: Writer's Digest Books, 1988. ISBN: 9780898793031.

Edgerton, Les. *Finding Your Voice: How to Put Personality in Your Writing*. Cincinnati: Writer's Digest Books, 2003. ISBN: 9781582971742.

Edgerton, Les. *Hooked: Write Fiction that Grabs Readers at Page One and Never Lets Them Go*. Cincinnati: Writer's Digest Books, 2007. ISBN: 9781582975146.

Evanovich, Janet with Ina Yalof. *How I Write: Secrets of a Bestselling Author*. New York: St. Martin's Griffin, 2006. ISBN: 9780312354282.

Frey, James N. *How to Write a Damn Good Novel: A Step-by-Step No Nonsense Guide to Dramatic Storytelling*. New York: St. Martin's Press, 1987. ISBN: 9780312010447.

Hemingway, Ernest. "Ernest Hemingway: Quotes. Quotable Quotes." Accessed October 23, 2024. www.goodreads.com/quotes/142038-we-are-all-apprentices-in-a-craft-where-no-one.

Hickman, Kirt. *Revising Fiction: Making Sense of the Madness*. Albuquerque: Quillrunner Publishing, LLC, 2009. ISBN: 9780979633010.

Gotham Writers' Workshop. *Writing Fiction: The Practical Guide from New York's Acclaimed Creative School*. New York: Bloomsbury, 2003. ISBN: 9781582343303.

Hansen, Joseph. "From the Writer Archive: The Ten Most Common Story Problems" (first published in *The Writer*, October 1976). *The Writer*, November 2008, 22-23, 54.

Hood, Ann. *Creating Character Emotions: Writing Compelling, Fresh Approaches that Express Your Character's True Feelings*. Cincinnati: Story Press, an imprint of F & W Publications, Inc., 1998. ISBN: 9781884910333.

Kempton, Gloria. "Fiction: Draft Better Dialogue." *Writer's Digest*, October 2006, 95-96.

Kempton, Gloria. *Dialogue: Techniques and Exercises for Crafting Effective Dialogue*. Write Great Fiction series. Cincinnati: Writer's Digest Books, 2004. ISBN: 9781582972893.

Kernen, Robert. *Building Better Plots*. Cincinnati: Writer's Digest Books, 1999. ISBN: 9780898799033.

King, Stephen. *On Writing: A Memoir of the Craft*. Paperback edition. New York: Pocket Books, 2000. ISBN: 9780671024253.

Kress, Nancy. *Characters, Emotion, and Viewpoint*. Write Great Fiction series. Cincinnati: Writer's Digest Books, 2005. ISBN: 9781582973166.

Kress, Nancy. *Dynamic Characters: How to Create Personalities that Keep Readers Captivated*. Cincinnati: Writer's Digest Books, 1998. ISBN: 9781582973197.

Kress, Nancy. "Fiction: Watch Your Tone!" *Writer's Digest*, July 2003, 16-18.

Kress, Nancy. "Make 'Em Think." *Writer's Digest*, August 2003, 38, 40-41.

Kress, Nancy. "Hold Them Back." *Writer's Digest*, August 2004, 42-45.

Kress, Nancy. "Fiction Essentials: The Inner Voice." *Writer's Digest*, March 2005, 14-15, 63.

Kress, Nancy. "Fiction Essentials: Exposition." *Writer's Digest*, May 2005, 22.

Kress, Nancy. "Fiction Essentials: Who Said That?" *Writer's Digest*, November 2005,

20-21.

Leonard, Elmore. *Elmore Leonard's 10 Rules of Writing*. New York: William Morrow, an imprint of HarperCollins Publishers, 2001. ISBN: 9780061451461.

Levin, Michael. "12 Random (but useful) Thoughts about Dialogue." *Writer's Digest*, January 2006, 34-37, 65.

Lukeman, Noah. *A Dash of Style: The Art and Mastery of Punctuation*. 1st paperback edition. New York: W. W. Norton & Company, 2006. ISBN: 9780393329803.

Lutz, Gary, and Diane Stevenson. *The Writer's Digest Grammar Desk Reference*. Cincinnati: Writer's Digest Books, 2005. ISBN: 9781582973357.

Maass, Donald. *Writing the Breakout Novel*. Cincinnati: Writer's Digest Books, 2001. ISBN: 9780898799958.

Maass, Donald. *The Fire in Fiction: Passion, Purpose, and Techniques to Make Your Novel Great*. Cincinnati: Writer's Digest Books, 2009. ISBN: 9781582975061.

Madden, David. "Creating Immediate, Urgent Stories," *Writer's Digest Handbook of Novel Writing*. Cincinnati: Writer's Digest Books, 1992.

Maifair, Linda Lee. "Story Dialogue." *Talk About*. Institute of Children's Literature, 1991, 1-4.

Marshall, Evan. *The Marshall Plan for Getting Your Novel Published: 90 Strategies and Techniques for Selling Your Fiction*. Cincinnati: Writer's Digest Books, 2003. ISBN: 9781582971964.

Marshall, Evan. *The Marshall Plan for Novel Writing: A 16-Step Program Guaranteed to Take You from Idea to Completed Manuscript*. Paperback edition. Cincinnati: Writer's Digest Books, 1998. ISBN: 9781582970622.

McPheat, Sean. "25 Learning and Development Quotes to Inspire You." Skillshub.com. Last modified March 5, 2024. https://www.skillshub.com/blog/learning-and-development-quotes/

Melville, Herman. *Moby-Dick*. New York: Barnes & Noble Classics, 2003. ISBN: 9781593080181.

Morrell, David. *Lessons from a Lifetime of Writing: A Novelist Looks at His Craft*. Cincinnati: Writer's Digest Books, 2002. ISBN: 9781582971438.

Morrell, Jessica Page. *Between the Lines: Master the Subtle Elements of Fiction Writing*. Cincinnati: Writer's Digest Books, 2006. ISBN: 9781582973937.

Plotnik, Arthur. *Spunk & Bite: A Writer's Guide to Bold, Contemporary Style*. Paperback edition. New York: Random House Reference, 2007. ISBN: 9780375722271.

Polking, Kirk, ed. *Writing A to Z: The Terms, Procedures, and Facts of the Writing Business Defined, Explained, and Put Within Reach*. Cincinnati: Writer's Digest Books, 1990. ISBN: 9780898794359.

Provost, Gary. *Beyond Style: Mastering the Finer Points of Writing*. Cincinnati: Writer's Digest Books, 1988. ISBN: 0898793149.

Rabin, Stanton. "Avoid a Weak Link in Screenplays." *The Writer*, March 2009, 36-38.

Rasley, Alicia. *The Power of Point of View: Make Your Story Come to Life.* Cincinnati: Writer's Digest Books, 2008. ISBN: 9781582975238.

Rosenfeld, Jordan E. *Make a Scene: Crafting a Powerful Story One Scene at a Time.* Cincinnati: Writer's Digest Books, 2008. ISBN: 9781582974798.

Reid, Mildred I. *The Writer's Digest Guide to Good Writing.* Cincinnati: Writer's Digest Books, 1994.

Rozelle, Ron. *Description and Setting: Techniques and Exercises for Crafting a Believable World of People, Places and Events.* Write Great Fiction series. Cincinnati: Writer's Digest Books, 2005. ISBN: 9781582973272.

Safire, William and Leonard Safire. *Good Advice on Writing: Writers Past and Present on How to Write Well.* New York: A Fireside Book, Simon & Schuster, 1992. ISBN: 9780671872335.

Scofield, Sandra. *The Scene Book: A Primer for the Fiction Writer.* New York: Penguin Books, 2007. ISBN: 9780143038269.

Selgin, Peter. *By Cunning & Craft: Sound Advice and Practical Wisdom for Fiction Writers.* Cincinnati: Writer's Digest Books, 2007. ISBN: 9781582974910.

Silvis, Randall. "From The Writer Archive: Let Your Dialogue Speak for Itself" (first published in February 1985). *The Writer,* March 2009, 24-25.

Sims, Elizabeth. "How to Make Your Novel a Page Turner." *Writer's Digest,* January 2010, 30-33.

Smith, James V. Jr. *You Can Write a Novel.* Cincinnati: Writer's Digest Books, 1998. ISBN: 9780898798685.

Stone, Todd A. *Novelist's Boot Camp: 101 Ways to Take Your Book from Boring to Bestseller.* Cincinnati: Writer's Digest Books, 2006. ISBN: 9781582973609.

Swain, Dwight V. *Techniques of the Selling Writer.* Norman, OK: University of Oklahoma Press, 1965. ISBN: 9780806111919.

Tapply, William G. "Step-by-Step: Dialogue: The Lifeblood of the Mystery Story." *The Writer,* October 2008, 30-33.

Truby, John. *Anatomy of a Story: 22 Steps to Becoming a Master Storyteller.* New York: Faber and Faber, Inc., 2007. ISBN: 9780865479517.

Watts, Nigel. *Teach Yourself: Writing a Novel.* Chicago: Contemporary Books, a division of McGraw-Hill Companies, 2003. ISBN: 9780071421058.

Whitney, Phyllis A. *Guide to Fiction Writing.* Boston: The Writer, Inc., 1982,1988. ISBN: 0871161575.

Wikipedia. http://en.wikipedia.org/wiki/.

ENDNOTES

PREFACE

1. Hemingway, Goodreads, Quotes.
2. King, *On Writing*, 11.

NOTE TO READERS

1. Marshall, *The Marshall Plan for Novel Writing*, 142.
2. Morrell, *Between the Lines*, 127.

1. SENSATION

1. Marshall, *The Marshall Plan for Getting Your Novel Published*, 16.
2. Rozelle, *Description and Setting*, 88.
3. Rozelle, *Description and Setting*, 88.
4. Rozelle, *Description and Setting*, 94.
5. Rozelle, *Description and Setting*, 88.
6. Marshall, *The Marshall Plan for Getting Your Novel Published*, 56-57.
7. Rozelle, *Description and Setting*, 78-95.
8. Stone, *Novelist's Boot Camp*, 235.
9. Rozelle, *Description and Setting*, 95-97.

2. EMOTION

1. Reid, *Writer's Digest Guide to Good Writing*, 105.
2. Kress, *Characters, Emotions, and Viewpoint*, 155.
3. Card, *Characters and Viewpoint*, 70.
4. Card, *Characters and Viewpoint*, 69.
5. Card, *Characters and Viewpoint*, 69.
6. Card, *Characters and Viewpoint*, 140.
7. Kress, *Characters, Emotions, and Viewpoint*, 147.
8. Hood, *Creating Character Emotion*, 18.
9. Kress, *Writer's Digest*, August 2004, 44.
10. Hood, *Creating Character Emotion*, 11.
11. Card, *Characters and Viewpoint*, 70.
12. Swain, *Techniques of the Selling Writer*, 84-90.
13. Swain, *Techniques of the Selling Writer*, 96-103.

3. INTROSPECTION

1. Kress, *Dynamic Characters*, 95-96.
2. Kress, *Writer's Digest*, March 2005, 63.
3. Bickham, *Scene & Structure*, 12.
4. Bickham, *Scene & Structure*, 17.
5. Bickham, *Scene & Structure*, 53-56.
6. Browne and King, *Self-Editing for Fiction Writers*, 126.
7. Kress, *Dynamic Characters*, 95.
8. Marshall, *The Marshall Plan for Getting Your Novel Published*, 44.
9. Marshall, *The Marshall Plan for Getting Your Novel Published*, 45.
10. Marshall, *The Marshall Plan for Getting Your Novel Published*, 44.
11. Kress, *Dynamic Characters*, 91-95.
12. Kress, *Dynamic Characters*, 91-95.

4. RECOLLECTION

1. Aristotle, *Poetics*, 13.
2. Card, *Characters & Viewpoint*, 113.

5. ACTION

1. Marshall, The Marshall Plan for Novel Writing, 142.
2. Whitney, *Guide to Fiction Writing*, 129.
3. Lutz and Stevenson, *The Writer's Digest Grammar Desk Reference*, 26-27, 30-31.
4. Swain, *Techniques of the Selling Writer*, 55.
5. Swain, *Techniques of the Selling Writer*, 55.
6. Browne and King, *Self-Editing for Fiction Writers*, 194.
7. Bickham, *Scene & Structure*, 14.
8. Marshall, *The Marshall Plan for Getting Your Novel Published*, 56-57.
9. Marshall, *The Marshall Plan for Getting Your Novel Published*, 56-57.

6. SUMMARIZATION

1. Marshall, *The Marshall Plan for Novel Writing, 144-145.*
2. Browne and King, *Self-Editing for Fiction Writers*, 14.

7. CONVERSATION

1. Kress, *Dynamic Characters*, 95.
2. Kress, *Dynamic Characters*, 95-96.
3. Rabin, *The Writer*, March 2009, 37.
4. Kempton, *Dialogue*, 167.

8. ADVANCING PLOT THROUGH ACTION AND DIALOGUE

1. Stone, *Novelist's Boot Camp*, 204-206.

9. DIALOGUE TO INCREASE CONFLICT

1. Kempton, *Dialogue*, 181.
2. Morrell, *Between the Lines*, 216.
3. Frey, *How to Write a Damned Good Novel*, 123.
4. Morrell, *Between the Lines*, 216.
5. Frey, *How to Write a Damned Good Novel, 123.*
6. Rosenfeld, *Make a Scene*, 164.
7. Selgin, *By Cunning & Craft*, 113.
8. Bell, *Plot & Structure*, 18.
9. Bell, *Plot & Structure*, 18.
10. Rosenfeld, *Make a Scene*, 164.
11. Chiarella, *Writing Dialogue, 29.*
12. Browne and King, *Self-Editing for Fiction Writers,* 104.
13. Browne and King, *Self-Editing for Fiction Writers,* 104.
14. Chiarella, *Writing Dialogue*, 31.
15. Chiarella, *Writing Dialogue*, 31.
16. Chiarella, *Writing Dialogue*, 31.
17. Hansen, *The Writer*, October 1976, 23.
18. Hansen, *The Writer*, October 1976, 23.
19. Rosenfeld, *Make a Scene*, 166.
20. Selgin, *By Cunning & Craft*, 112.
21. Rosenfeld, *Make a Scene*, 166.
22. Gotham Writers' Workshop, *Writing Fiction*, 144.
23. Kempton, *Writer's Digest*, October 2006, 96.

10. IDENTIFYING THE SPEAKER

1. Browne and King, *Self-Editing for Fiction Writers, 92.*
2. Levin, *Writer's Digest,* January 2006, 36.
3. Levin, *Writer's Digest,* January 2006, 36.
4. Levin, *Writer's Digest,* January 2006, 36.
5. Marshall, *The Marshall Plan for Novel Writing*, 149.
6. Maifair, "Story Dialogue," 2.
7. Maifair, "Story Dialogue," 2.

11. VERBS AND ADVERBS OF ATTRIBUTION

1. Chiarella, *Writing Dialogue*, 131.
2. Bickham, *38 Common Fiction Writing Mistakes*, 54.
3. Chiarella, *Writing Dialogue*, 133.
4. Melville, *Moby-Dick*, 551.
5. Chiarella, *Writing Dialogue*, 131.
6. Morrell, *Lessons from a Lifetime of Writing*, 155.
7. Morrell, *Lessons from a Lifetime of Writing*, 154.
8. Selgin, *By Cunning & Craft*, 109.

12. USING ATTRIBUTIONS TO CONTROL RHYTHM AND PACE

1. Chiarella, *Writing Dialogue*, 132.
2. Morrell, *Lessons from a Lifetime of Writing*, 160.
3. Morrell, *Lessons from a Lifetime of Writing*, 160.

13. MAKING DIALOGUE SOUND NATURAL

1. Hansen, *The Writer* (first published October 1976), reprinted November 2009, 23.
2. Tapply, *The Writer*, October 2008, 30.
3. Bell, *The Artful Edit*, 124.
4. Truby, *Anatomy of a Story*, 377.
5. Kress, *Characters, Emotion, and Viewpoint*, 117.
6. Bickham, *38 Common Fiction Writing Mistakes*, 47.
7. Bickham, *38 Common Fiction Writing Mistakes*, 47.
8. Browne and King, *Self-Editing for Fiction Writers*, 101.
9. Selgin, *By Cunning & Craft*, 105.
10. Kempton, "Fiction: Draft Better Dialogue: How to recognize bad dialogue," *Writer's Digest*, 96.
11. Marshall, *The Marshall Plan for Novel Writing*, 153.

14. PUNCTUATING DIALOGUE

1. Chicago Manual of Style, 13.50.
2. Chicago Manual of Style, 13.55.
3. Chicago Manual of Style, 13.53
4. Chicago Manual of Style, 9.2.
5. Chicago Manual of Style, 9.4.
6. Chicago Manual of Style, 9.5.
7. Chicago Manual of Style, 543-569.
8. Chiarella, *Writing Dialogue*, 148.

15. NARRATION

1. Card, *Characters & Viewpoint*, 140.

16. DESCRIPTION

1. Swain, *Techniques of the Selling Writer*, 25.
2. Swain, *Techniques of the Selling Writer*, 26.
3. Selgin, *By Cunning & Craft*, 136.
4. Swain, *Techniques of the Selling Writer*, 31.
5. Swain, *Techniques of the Selling Writer*, 31.
6. Wikipedia, "Intensifier."
7. Wikipedia, "Intensifier."
8. Wikipedia, "Intensifier."
9. Wikipedia, "Expletive."
10. Wikipedia, "Expletive."
11. Wikipedia, "Expletive."
12. Wikipedia, "Figure of Speech."
13. Wikipedia, "Figure of Speech."
14. Wikipedia, "Figure of Speech."
15. Wikipedia, "Extended Metaphor."
16. Wikipedia, "All the World's a Stage."
17. Swain, *Techniques of the Selling Writer*, 34.

17. EXPOSITION

1. Safire, *Good Advice on Writing*, 122.
2. Kress, *Writer's Digest*, May 2005, 23.
3. Dibell, *Plot*, 49.
4. Bickham, *Scene & Structure*, 55.
5. Dibell, *Plot*, 56.

18. TRANSITION

1. Morrell, *Between the Lines*, 282.
2. Morrell, *Between the Lines*, 283.
3. Lukeman, *A Dash of Style*, 159.
4. Marshall, *The Marshall Plan for Novel Writing*, 137.
5. Madden, *Writer's Digest Handbook of Novel Writing*, 162.
6. Morrell, *Between the Lines*, 289.
7. Morrell, *Between the Lines*, 288.
8. Morrell, *Between the Lines*, 291.
9. Morrell, *Between the Lines*, 291.

Made in United States
Troutdale, OR
02/04/2025